Beyond Sustainability Reporting

Beyond Sustainability Reporting

The Pathway to Corporate Social Responsibility

Gerald Trites

BUSINESS EXPERT PRESS

Leader in applied, concise business books

Beyond Sustainability Reporting: The Pathway to Corporate Social Responsibility

First published in 2024 by
Business Expert Press, LLC
222 East 46th Street, New York, NY 10017
www.businessexpertpress.com

ISBN-13: 978-1-63742-618-0 (paperback)
ISBN-13: 978-1-63742-619-7 (e-book)

Business Expert Press Financial Accounting, Auditing, and Taxation Collection

First edition: 2024

10 9 8 7 6 5 4 3 2 1

Description

How to Convert Sustainability Disclosure Into Action

New standards such as those of the International Sustainability Standards Board and new regulations from the Securities and Exchange Commission are challenging companies to increase and improve their disclosure on what they are doing to support sustainability for their environmental, social, and governance activities.

Companies are responding by changing their controls and procedures to include sustainability processes. But is this enough?

For companies that truly want to help with sustainability issues, the answer is *no*.

What *is* needed is the more action-oriented approach laid out in this book, which:

- Enables modifying the corporate strategic plans to include real sustainability actions;
- Makes use of the skills developed in providing sustainability disclosures, such as integrated thinking;
- Includes proper adoption of recognized standards for control procedures recognized by regulatory authorities;
- Adapts traditional management change tools, such as SWOT and Porter's Five Forces Model to include sustainability; and
- Shows how to move the company from sustainability disclosure to integrated thinking to corporate social responsibility.

Beyond Sustainability Reporting: The Pathway to Corporate Social Responsibility is a must-read for any company wanting to make a strong contribution to sustainability issues, for educators who wish to teach sustainability issues and how to manage them, and for anyone interested in knowing how companies can develop a strong and successful action-oriented program for sustainability.

Keywords

how to develop sustainability strategy; corporate social responsibility; meeting the United Nations' SDGs; how to transition from sustainability to corporate social responsibility; sustainability disclosures; how to develop a corporate social responsibility strategy; how to incorporate CSR in your strategic planning; using integrated thinking; ESG reporting

Contents

Preface

Climate change is a reality for most people, along with issues like equality, diversity, and corporate governance. Corporate reporting and management have been responding to these issues with new rules, requirements, and actions under the label of sustainability reporting, previously ESG reporting. This field is expanding rapidly despite the views of some who find ESG reporting to be objectionable.

This book addresses these issues directly, pointing out not only that sustainability reporting is essential but that it is not enough—that sustainability needs to be integrated into the strategies and management of companies through the adoption of corporate social responsibility (CSR) programs. It also outlines how this can be accomplished. Further, it argues that CSR does not endanger profitability but instead supports it. This is important for people to understand.

My thanks to Alex Young, FCA, FCPA; Don Sheehy, CPA, CA; and David Wray, noted author, for reviewing the manuscript and providing me with their excellent comments. Of course, all remaining shortcomings and errors are my responsibility.

I also thank my very bright and talented wife, Margaret MacDonald Trites, for her proof-reading, help, and support which she always unhesitatingly and cheerfully provides.

Gerald Trites

CHAPTER 1

Introduction

There are few things more important to the welfare of humanity in this early 21st century than the state of the environment. Although large segments of the scientific community have been warning us for years about the effects of climate change, a growing concern about the environment has been prompted by the effects of extreme weather events over recent years.

Some progress is being made. The 2023 United Nations Climate Change Conference or Conference of the Parties, more commonly known as COP28, was held in December 2023 in Dubai. It was an important year in the battle against climate change. Nearly 200 nations agreed to begin "transitioning away from fossil fuels"—the first-ever climate accord to address this primary driver of warming temperatures. In addition, more than 20 countries from four continents launched a declaration to triple nuclear energy, thus recognizing the key role of nuclear energy in achieving global net-zero objectives.

Companies Can Take Action

Companies have been disclosing their sustainability efforts for years but more recently have been pressured to take stronger action on concerns about the environment and climate-related issues, as well as social and corporate governance issues. For example, social issues, which involve how a company manages its relationships with society generally, and customers and suppliers in particular, have been at the forefront for growing numbers of people. And governance issues, including issues around executive pay, equality, inclusiveness, and diversity, have all been the center of widespread concern.

While there is legislation attempting to address some of these issues, governments have been finding it difficult to take strong action because of social and political polarization and uncertainties about how to proceed. The UN resolution is helping tremendously. But more importantly, there is a growing realization that corporations have the power to accomplish a great deal without the help or prompting of governments. Companies have indeed been responding with stronger sustainability reporting and also with strategic and managerial changes in their operations to improve upon their environmental footprint. But while there have been some exemplary cases, the response has not always been effective. Sustainability reports have often been selective and vague, greenwashing and glossing over the real issues.

Because of the frequent inconsistencies and vagueness in sustainability reports, stakeholders developed an interest in establishing standards and consolidating existing ones. Ultimately, this led to the formation of international standards-setting bodies, notably the International Sustainability Standards Board (ISSB), which has been charged with issuing global standards for sustainability reporting primarily directed to shareholders and intended to ensure comparability, relevance, and balanced, objective reporting.

In the past, when the question of addressing sustainability issues was raised, business people often stated a view that this was inconsistent with their prime objective, to make profits. Therefore, this book begins with an exploration of the role of profit in corporations now and in the past, how this is shifting to a greater emphasis on sustainable business models, and how profit has normally been a means to an end rather than an end in itself.

While sustainability reporting is important, we need to move beyond that to changing the fundamental ways we carry on business. This book is about how corporations (and other businesses and organizations) can move from sustainability reporting to a more comprehensive approach to meeting their social responsibilities without sacrificing their economic viability or, indeed, without sacrificing profits at all.

The Meaning of Sustainability

While sustainability is the more common term being used today, in the past it was more common to talk about ESG. ESG refers to Environmental, Social, and Governance:

The **Environmental** element concerns how a business performs as a steward of our natural environment. It focuses on:

- waste and pollution
- resource depletion
- greenhouse gas emission
- deforestation
- climate change

The **Social** element looks at how the company interacts with people and concentrates on:

- employee relations and diversity
- working conditions, including child labor and slavery
- local communities; for example, funding projects or institutions that will serve poor and underserved communities
- health and safety
- conflict

Governance involves the structure and processes a company uses to police itself—how the company is governed—and focuses on:

- tax strategy
- executive remuneration
- donations and political lobbying
- corruption and bribery
- board diversity and structure[*]

The Environmental Element

For years, scientists have warned us about the likelihood of a major climate crisis, disruptions, calamities, and even the end of life as we know it. People have reacted in different ways, some with action or concern, some with skepticism and others with obstinance and rebellion: a full

---

[*] https://marketbusinessnews.com/financial-glossary/esg-definition-meaning/.

range of normal human reactions. Organizations have sprung up to combat the threat, and governments have discussed the possibility of initiatives to address it. While some businesses have acted responsibly, taking strong action to reduce their footprint on the climate, others have reacted with some, often limited, initiatives designed to convey the message that they are not ignoring the issue. Still others ignored the issue. Schools and universities have introduced new courses and programs. But in the minds of some, the reality of climate change, and in particular, climate change caused by human activity, was all speculative for many years.

And then reality began to hit us with extreme heat waves, massive floods, and sometimes unmanageable forest and brush fires. The years 2022–2023 were the worst so far.

In the United Kingdom, land of wools and cool, misty moors, temperatures reached 40°C (110°F) in 2022 for the first time in recorded history. The American Southwest suffered with 40°C (110°F) plus temperatures for months. Icebergs at both poles calved with unprecedented regularity, and in August 2022, the melting of the Greenland glaciers was pronounced irreversible by some scientists, with a consequent projected rise in sea levels of 27 cm by the century's end. Twenty-seven centimeters (about 11 in.) may not sound like much, but the fact is when you take into account the compounding effects of waves and wind and strong storm surges, it will create extensive flooding in many areas of the world and numerous cities. And pronouncements were made by the World Economic Forum (WEF) and others that some areas in the world, because of flooding and extreme heat, would soon become uninhabitable by humans, including parts of the Middle East, India, and Bangladesh.

As this book is being written, the year 2023 is shaping up to be just as bad—or worse. The record books show that 2023 has been the warmest year on record, based on data up to August. Canadian forests are burning with record ferocity and the smoke has been covering a major part of the North American continent, with smoke alarms raised in cities such as New York, Toronto, Chicago, and Boston. In mid-2023, some of the Greek Islands were evacuated because of wildfires.

Widespread smoke from the Canadian wildfires in much of 2023 created hazardous air quality across the U.S. Northeast and Mid-Atlantic in particular. For several days, New York City and Washington were covered in thick smoke with severe consequences for anyone attempting to breathe the air. Wildfires in the west, particularly in California and British Columbia, have continued to devastate those communities.

Also, in August 2023, the United States experienced its worst-ever wildfire on the Hawaiian island of Maui, where the historic capital of Lahaina was destroyed with a significant loss of life.

In 2023, the National Oceanic and Atmospheric Administration (NOAA) of the United States reported that between 1980 and 2020, the United States has sustained 323 weather and climate disasters since 1980 where overall damages/costs reached or exceeded one billion dollars. **The total cost of these 323 events exceeded \$2.570 trillion.**[†]

In 2023, NOAA also reported that, as of July 11, there were 12 confirmed weather/climate disaster events with losses exceeding one billion dollars each to affect the United States. These events included 1 flooding event, 10 severe storm events, and 1 winter storm event. Overall, these events resulted in the deaths of 100 people and had significant economic effects on the areas impacted. The 1980 to 2022 annual average is 8.1 events; the annual average for the most recent five years (2018–2022) is 18.0 events.

These events and their devastating effects on business began to raise awareness in the minds of corporate leaders that the climate could have an adverse impact on business sooner than they thought. Attitudes began to change, importantly those of the stakeholders to whom companies must be held accountable. So, many business leaders have begun to take a new interest in sustainability.

It was mostly the extreme weather that captured the attention of the boardrooms in the country. It became obvious that, without taking any action, extreme weather events would be detrimental to the companies and the economy. As physical assets were burned and flooded, legal issues arose and business activities suffered. Corporate boards and management were forced to come to grips with at least some of the environmental effects of climate change.

[†] www.ncei.noaa.gov/news/calculating-cost-weather-and-climate-disasters.

Some actions were easy to identify. If a factory near the ocean experienced regular flooding in storms, then it became obvious that it would need to be moved or replaced. If a new facility were planned, then the potential of damage from major climate events would have to be taken into account in its design and location. Pressure grew against the use of fossil fuels, with a recognition that new types of fuel would eventually have to be used. Tesla introduced the electric car, followed by most major car manufacturers, and despite fears that they were not yet ready for general use, they became more popular, especially in Europe. In August of 2022, the California Air Resources Board (CARB) said it would require, by 2035, all new vehicles sold in California to be electric or plug-in hybrids. But electric vehicles have their limitations (range, battery availability, and durability), and we may find that they are not sustainable either, unless the technology advances quickly to overcome these limitations.

As companies began to consider their carbon footprint, they began changing to solar and hydraulic power. The rise of the "net carbon zero" mantra followed quickly, with many companies declaring they would reach that milestone by the year 2050, the deadline year designated by the Paris Agreement.[‡] On the face of it, progress was being made.

In related areas, such as garbage and waste disposal, more apparent progress had been made for years. Invocations such as "recycle, reuse, reduce" had been taught to students from grade school up for many years. Afterward, we evolved from this 70s idea to "refuse or reduce, reuse," and only if those cannot be done, then we recycle. Recycling had become a normal part of life in many parts of the world. We were asked to sort all our garbage into paper, plastic, compost, and just plain garbage. Sadly, too much of the plastic ended up in the oceans in various ways. But at least we felt we were doing something about the problem.

[‡] The Paris Agreement is a legally binding international treaty on climate change. It was adopted by 196 Parties at the UN Climate Change Conference (COP21) in Paris, France, on December 12, 2015. It entered into force on November 4, 2016. See also The United Nations Climate Change Website. https://unfccc.int/process-and-meetings/the-paris-agreement.

The Social Element

The social component of sustainability addresses how a company manages its relations with its employees, contractors, suppliers, investors, creditors, community, and the political environment. It's beneficial for companies to be regarded as good employers and responsible corporate citizens.

To meet their social responsibilities, companies often promote an "inclusive culture" in their organization. They feature diversity, equity, and inclusion. They also strive to improve their employees' experience through performance management, reward systems, recognition, employee satisfaction, and assistance with mental health, stress, and parenting. Work-life balance has been a major issue for years, but the concept has been upended because of the pandemic, which led to the introduction of modified styles of working, from home, off-site, and hybrid work. As the pandemic slowed down, there was some retraction from the pandemic styles of working, but the retreat has so far been a lot less than complete. It became apparent that work and life were becoming more closely entangled because of the work-from-home model. The work-life idea has always been somewhat flawed because of the fact that, for many, work is a major component of "life" and the two are not completely separable. However, the term was widely accepted as a proxy for a search for a better balance in life.

Social justice is very much related to equality and inequality between people. Inequality has been a major factor leading to unrest in much of human history, which is traced diligently by the economist Thomas Piketty. He points out that inequality remains a prominent reality in today's society. But he argues that over the long span of time, equality has improved very slowly all around the world. Nevertheless, we still see inequality in the major gaps that have developed between the incomes of the working class and those of the 1 percent and the ruling or governing classes. Much data is available to support this. For example, "according to a 2022 Credit Suisse report, 47.8 percent of global household wealth is in the hands of just 1.2 percent of the world's population. Those 62.5 million individuals control a staggering $221.7 trillion."[§]

[§] www.statista.com/chart/11857/the-global-pyramid-of-wealth/.

The Governance Element

The governance element of sustainability recognizes that corporate governance is a complex influence on the broad spectrum of developmental issues. Governance includes political strategies, management, and leadership. It includes the organization through which the principles of governance are applied, such as management structures, the board of directors and related committees, and executives in the C-Suite. The basic purpose of sustainable government must be to protect and promote the best interests of the stakeholders. It is necessary that government invest in strategies that promote sustainable development.

Governance has drawn attention to issues, among others, around executive compensation: why are CEOs paid more in the first few days of the year than the average worker earns in a year, which also relates to the issue of inequality. Companies have also been taking more action (some would say not enough) on placing women and ethnic minorities on boards and ethics training to educate management and directors so that they can better support an ethical work environment and, generally, human rights. Legislation has been passed in several countries to support and enforce diversity.

Sustainability in Business Strategy

Significant change is underway in the thinking of corporate executives, in how they plan strategy and how they manage. Their objectives are broadening and moving beyond the sole primacy of profitability. The change is taking place in local, regional, and global businesses.

While profits will always be important, they are becoming part of an overall set of objectives in which they will remain an important part but will have to share the stage with other factors, such as environmental, social, and governmental considerations.

Sustainability was defined in 1987 by the United Nations Brundtland Commission as "consisting of fulfilling the needs of current generations without compromising the needs of future generations, while ensuring a balance between economic growth, environmental care, and social well-being."[5] Much of the discourse about sustainability has been focused on the environmental impacts of organizations, but there is extensive writing and research on the much broader concept of social and governance issues as well as such elements as

> Make's six principles of sustainability— Carbon, Environment, Community, Wellbeing, Connectivity, and Green economy. These principles are guided from concept to completion by the RIBA 2030 Climate Challenge, the LETI Climate Emergency Design Guide, and the UN Sustainable Development Goals (SDGs).

The point is that sustainability has become a broad and somewhat diverse concept.

Integrated Reporting and Thinking

In the area of corporate reporting, most companies that report on sustainability present the information in a separate report. However, the growing realization that investors have a particular interest in sustainability because of the impact on financial affairs, either now or in the future, has led to some re-evaluation of this approach. This led to the concept of integrated reporting, in which sustainability information is integrated with financial information. Full integration, as opposed to just presenting information side by side, requires a change in mindset by the preparers of those reports, usually the finance department and the public relations arm of the company. In order to facilitate integrated reporting, the concept of integrated thinking emerged, which takes the next natural step in the development of corporate strategy to support integrated reporting. Integrated thinking means the company considers sustainability factors along with financial factors not only in doing their reports but also in carrying out strategy, policies, and planning and execution. This would involve not only finance but a wide swath of the company personnel and departments and perhaps external specialists, as needed.

---

[5] www.un.org/en/academic-impact/sustainability.

Implementation of integrated thinking requires cultural change, which can only happen with the involvement and support of a wide range of personnel in the company, including leadership and a supportive tone at the top. Education and discussion are necessary to achieve cultural change.

Corporate Social Responsibility

When corporations reach acceptance of sustainability as a business objective along with profit and growth, they will need to decide whether and how to proceed from there. A strong possibility is the adoption of corporate social responsibility (CSR), particularly strategic corporate social responsibility, which involves embedding CSR into the strategic planning of a company. It's similar in some ways to integrated thinking in that it involves including sustainability strategies in major corporate decisions, but it differs by supporting a broader range of activities than corporate reporting. CSR subsumes the idea of corporate reporting and focuses on overall corporate behavior. This is the logical outcome of adopting integrated thinking and reporting and sets the stage for a new era in the role of corporations in society, one that sets a much greater emphasis on doing good for society, not at the expense of profits, because they will always be necessary, but with the good done in such a way as to augment the profits. It leads to a focus on how profits are made, as opposed to how much profit is made.

CHAPTER 2

Pressures on Corporate Behavior

Companies must respond to the pressures placed upon them to change their behavior by their stakeholders, which include investors, customers, suppliers, employees, and sometimes the general public. These pressures encompass the company's effect on the environment, to help preserve it, or at least to disclose their effect on the environment and the effects of the environment on them in their annual or sustainability reports. There are also pressures to adopt some kind of social responsibility policy and to disclose pertinent details of their governance policies. This includes their stance on diversity, particularly the gender representations on their boards, and in management.

Stakeholder activism has gained momentum in recent years. Social media and online platforms provide individuals with a powerful voice to call out companies for perceived injustices, misleading advertising, or unethical behavior. Consumers are increasingly willing to support or boycott brands based on their own values, forcing companies to be more responsive and accountable. Society expects companies to go beyond profit making and actively contribute to social and environmental causes. Businesses are often expected to engage in social responsibility initiatives, such as philanthropy, community development programs, or sustainability projects, to demonstrate their commitment to the well-being of society. Some companies have done this for years, but the pressure has grown on all companies to do so.

Most of these pressures originate in a desire for environmental sustainability, addressing of social issues, and maintenance of good ethical behavior.

Environmental Sustainability

With growing concerns about climate change and environmental degradation, companies face increasing pressure to adopt sustainable practices. Stakeholders expect businesses to minimize their environmental footprint, reduce greenhouse gas emissions, and conserve natural resources. Companies that are seen as disregarding these concerns may face boycotts, regulatory hurdles, and reputational damage. For example, growing concerns about plastic pollution have led to societal pressure on companies to reduce their plastic usage. In response, many companies have implemented strategies such as using recycled or biodegradable packaging, offering reusable alternatives, or promoting refillable options.

As an example, it's been over a decade since General Electric launched Ecomagination, its renewable business strategy with a mission to double down on clean technology and generate $20 billion in revenue from green products. As part of its "Ecomagination Challenge,"[*] the 2023 Challenge was launched in July to accelerate the development of the next-generation power grid. The challenge generated nearly 4,000 ideas and involved 70,000 entrepreneurs in more than 150 countries. The five winners received $100,000 each. The winning ideas were (1) a lightweight inflatable wind turbine; (2) a technology that instantly de-ices wind turbine blades so they never slow or shut down; (3) an intelligent water meter that can generate its own power; (4) a cyber-secure network infrastructure that allows two-way communications grid monitoring and substation automation from wind and solar farms; and (5) a technology that solves short-circuiting and outages from overloaded electric grids by enabling precise control over their flow and power. This program is an important contribution to environmental sustainability.

As another example, Parley for the Oceans is a global environmental organization where creators, thinkers, and leaders come together to raise awareness of the beauty and fragility of the oceans and collaborate on projects that can help end their destruction. In 2018, Adidas partnered with Parley to make shoes out of recycled plastics scavenged from the

---

[*] https://digitalmarketinginstitute.com/blog/corporate-16-brands-doing-corporate-social-responsibility-successfully.

ocean. Parley collects the plastic from beaches and Adidas breaks it down into usable material. Each shoe in the Parley collection is made from at least 75 percent intercepted marine trash.[†]

The push for sustainable energy solutions and concerns about climate change also have driven pressure on companies to transition to renewable energy sources. Many businesses have committed to using renewable energy for their operations, investing in renewable energy projects, or setting ambitious targets to reduce their carbon emissions.

Social Issues

Businesses are expected to operate in ways that benefit society at large, such as promoting diversity and inclusion, ensuring fair labor practices, and contributing positively to local communities. Failure to meet these expectations can lead to public backlash, damaged reputation, and potential loss of customers. Under pressure, some organizations have implemented diversity programs, set targets for the representation of under-represented groups, and taken steps to address pay gaps and unconscious bias in their hiring and promotion practices. While this issue is often hard to define, it is extremely important for businesses to understand the potential impact of diversity. New research from the World Economic Forum and Accenture shows that 59 percent of people who identify with a racial and ethnic minority tend to engage with brands more frequently if they are inclusive of diverse perspectives. Just over half (51 percent) of women are more likely to trust brands that represent a diverse range of people.

There is legislation related to most of the areas of employee relations and diversity, working conditions, child labor and slavery, impact on local communities, and health and safety, but legislation generally sets minimum standards. There is scope for companies to go beyond the minimum standards, but if they do, the extent varies from company to company. The areas of employee relations and diversity are good examples. While much progress has been made in recent years, particularly with regard to diversity, much more needs to be done. Laws around diversity and discrimination have helped, but cultural change and education are needed to further the transition.

[†] www.sustainablebusinesstoolkit.com/examples-corporate-social-responsibility/.

The experience of the pandemic and its aftermath have taught us something about this issue. Many of the lower-paying jobs in our society are those of the service industry, such as restaurants, hotels, airlines, and so on. Many of them are paid minimum wage or close to it and depend on irregular hours with little or no benefits. When the COVID-19 pandemic started, many of them were laid off. When restrictions were lifted, the companies tried to hire them back, but a lot of them didn't come back. The big question of the time was "Where have all the workers gone?" We know now that many of them changed their line of work, often taking additional training and gaining new skills with better paying and more reliable employment. Some came back after their government support payments ended. Some simply went into retirement, a function of the large numbers of baby boomers in the workforce. Some employers began to understand that they would need to work harder to retain people, perhaps by raising wages and offering more benefits. Also diversity became more important for rebuilding the workforce.

In a strategy to diversify its workforce, Starbucks pledged to hire 25,000 U.S. military veterans and spouses by 2025. The company reached this milestone six years early and now hires 5,000 veterans and spouses per year. In addition, to address racial and social equity, Starbucks announced

a mentorship program to connect black, indigenous, and people of color to senior leaders and invest in partnerships. The chain also aims to have black, indigenous, and people of color represented at 30 percent in corporate roles and 40 percent in retail and manufacturing by 2025.[‡]

Employees, especially the new and younger ones, are becoming more vocal about their expectations of their employers. They seek organizations that align with their values and provide a positive work environment. Companies that do not prioritize employee well-being, diversity, or work-life balance will struggle to attract and retain top talent. In addition, governments worldwide are enacting stricter regulations to address societal concerns.

[‡] https://digitalmarketinginstitute.com/blog/corporate-16-brands-doing-corporate-social-responsibility-successfully.

These regulations can range from labor and human rights standards to environmental protection laws. Companies that do not comply with these regulations may face fines, legal repercussions, and negative public perception.

Pfizer, a major pharmaceutical company, has a fundamental and critical stake in health care and provides a good example of moving beyond regulatory and legal requirements. They have a strategy to respond to disasters with a three-pronged approach: product donations, grants, and solutions to access. In 2022, they were named "one of the most ethical companies in the world by Ethisphere."[§] Grants were provided to countries such as Haiti in the aftermath of Hurricane Matthew and to others in Europe and the Middle East to help address the refugee crisis. During the COVID-19 pandemic, Pfizer provided five million dollars to help improve the recognition, diagnosis, treatment, and management of patients. In addition, grants were made available to clinics, medical centers, and hospitals to improve the management and outcome of COVID-19 patients.

Ethical Business Practices

Society is becoming more vigilant about ethical conduct in business. Companies are expected to uphold high ethical standards throughout their operations, including responsible sourcing, transparency in supply chains, and fair treatment of employees. Unethical practices, such as exploitative labor conditions or involvement in corruption, within the company or in their supply chains, can lead to public outrage, legal consequences, and loss of consumer trust. Increased awareness of unethical labor practices in global supply chains has led to demands for greater transparency. Companies are being pressured to disclose information about their suppliers, ensure fair wages and safe working conditions, and address issues such as child labor and human rights abuses.

There has been a rise in demand for ethically produced goods, such as fair-trade products or items sourced from environmentally responsible suppliers. Companies that fail to meet these expectations risk losing customers to competitors who prioritize and communicate their emphasis on ethical considerations.

---

§ Ibid.

Ethics is an important part of the social pressures on companies. Common ethical issues include:

- *Unethical Leadership in General*: Other ethical issues related to corporate governance include—executive remuneration, accountability, conflicts of interest and transparency. All involve discretion by the board and are key aspects of ethical behavior within the boardroom, as well as being issues which boards need to address for their organizations.
- *Toxic Workplace Culture*: According to the Ethics & Compliance Initiative's 2018 Global Benchmark on Workplace Ethics, 30 percent of employees in the United States personally observed misconduct in the past 12 months, a number close to the global median for misconduct observation. There is a cost to unethical practices.
- *Questionable Use of Company Technology*: This can range from using company computers for personal purposes to unauthorized downloading of corporate data and using it for nonbusiness purposes. Concerns about data privacy and cybersecurity have pushed companies to enhance their practices in safeguarding user information. Data breaches and privacy violations have resulted in public outcry, leading to increased demands for stronger data protection measures and transparent data-handling practices.
- *Discrimination*: This is one of the biggest ethical issues affecting the business world in 2020. It usually involves members of minority groups but also can involve disadvantaged individuals, on a physical or mental basis.
- *Harassment*: Closely related to toxic workplaces, harassment can come from bullying, discrimination, aggressive or insensitive managers, and individual rivalry among personnel.
- *Unethical or Inappropriate Accounting*: There have been many examples over recent years. Some of these have led to accusations that the auditors failed to do their job, which have caught the attention of the audit overseers, such as the Public

Company Accounting Oversight Board (PCAOB) along with the securities regulators such as the SEC and OSC.

- Ethics has a particularly strong effect on audit firms. They must conduct their audits in accordance with established standards, such as generally accepted assurance standards and generally accepted accounting principles. Their codes of ethics encompass compliance with these standards, and the auditors can be charged with ethical violations such as lack of integrity. This is at the core of their work, and since auditors without integrity are not of any use to the business world, it can put them out of business.

- *Health and Safety*: Provision of proper health and wellness standards for personnel can be a legal issue and often is, but it is always an ethical issue as well. It can lead to illness and even death. There are many examples, but one could be the dangers of asbestos in buildings. Although they have been known for many years, there are still older buildings with asbestos in them. There are many instances of management ignoring and hiding the fact that a building contains asbestos, causing harm to their personnel, sometimes cancer and death.

- *Abuse of Leadership Authority*: Power corrupts, and there are many examples of high-level leadership abusing their authority and perhaps lack of oversight to obtain inappropriate personal gains.

- *Nepotism and Favoritism*: Nepotism is usually easy to spot and is often called out by others in an organization or overseers. However, it is common in privately owned companies and often an accepted part of organizational behavior, where control of companies is handed down to sons and daughters. Favoritism is much more difficult to identify and control. Good attention to ethical standards and enforcement thereof is the most effective solution to this behavior.

- *Privacy*: Violation of privacy has been a major target of new legislation in recent years. Privacy acts exist in most Western economies, which restrict the use and distribution of names and contact information without permission. However, a large concern has been the exposure of individuals to having their private information given to a company through hacking and virus attacks. Numerous incidents of such attacks have made the news headlines, leading to accusations that the company involved did not do enough to protect the privacy of the people whose information they held in their databases, such as information of employees, customers, debtors and creditors, and others with whom the company has done business.

• *Corporate Espionage*: Often practiced by companies to gain competitive advantage, corporate espionage is sometimes taken to extreme levels where the rights of others to privacy are violated.

Investors are recognizing the importance of sustainability and responsible corporate practices. They are increasingly incorporating sustainability criteria into their investment decisions. Companies that fail to address these concerns will face difficulty attracting investment capital, leading to reduced growth opportunities and decreased shareholder value.

To navigate these pressures effectively, companies are recognizing the need to adapt their strategies, policies, and practices. Embracing sustainable and ethical business models, engaging in transparent communication, and actively listening to stakeholders are essential steps toward meeting societal expectations and ensuring long-term success. Societal pressures can drive companies to re-evaluate their practices, make changes to align with societal expectations, and ultimately improve their reputation and long-term sustainability.

Many of these pressures and challenges arose in the modern environment of rapid transmission of news and social media. But they did not start there. The seeds of change we are experiencing today were grounded in changes in corporate behavior that took place during the 20th century.

Corporate Change in the Late 20th Century

During the 1980s, a major shift took place in the business world, particularly in that part of it represented by large companies. That was the time of megamergers, when KKR merged with Nabisco, Warner with Time, Texaco with Getty, and so on. It was also the era when mergers led to conglomerates—organizations with very different lines of business having little apparent relationship to each other. Those included mergers like U.S. Steel and Marathon Oil, BA Tobacco and Farmers Insurance, Eastman Kodak and Sterling Drug, Sony and Columbia Pictures. These examples were mergers of just two businesses, but true conglomerates, with numerous lines of business developed from such beginnings, like Berkshire Hathaway, United Technologies and Dow Chemical. It was the time of corporate raiders and Gordon Gekko's "Greed is good" speech.[1]

Many companies expanded through mergers in different countries to become multinationals and multinational conglomerates, accelerating the growth of the global economy. These shifts in business reflected shifts in business strategy, with one of the major ones being an increased emphasis on profits. For many years before that time, companies were often devoted to developing and selling a single product or line of related products. This has an effect on management objectives. When a single product is developed and sold, management has a very strong incentive to emphasize the quality of that product. Profits are important, but management's attitudes reflect the fact that the very existence of the company depends on the success and quality of that product. If that product fails, then chances are the company may also fail.

On the other hand, if many products are sold, then the loss of a single product is less likely to be life-threatening. The commitment to the quality of a product is watered down. Management's strategic emphasis will be less on product quality and more on profits. This emphasis on profits was supported by the attitudes of investors, who are keen to maximize their return on investment. This leads to an emphasis on short-term results. Companies that meet the short-term expectations of analysts are rewarded, and those who fall short are penalized. These are underlying trends that shape the performance of the stock markets. Loss of market value can have a detrimental effect on the ability of the company to raise capital.

The increased emphasis on profits made it more difficult to convince companies to concern themselves about the environment. The question was always, if we adopt restrictive measures to control our impact on the environment, will it hurt profitability? Or by how much will it reduce profits? Early pressures on companies to reduce their impact on the environment, therefore, often fell on deaf ears until the more recent attention by stakeholders to sustainability matters and extreme climate events led some companies to shift their business objectives.

The growth of multinational companies also led to the advent of globalization, where companies can operate in different countries largely of their choosing. As a result, they can choose countries with less restrictive laws and customs and more favorable tax environments, thus enabling them to pay less attention to sustainability factors. Regulators such as the SEC have long ago established rules around ethics in dealing with other countries; however, in many cases, companies have managed to escape some of the pressures from their own countries and even their shareholders. This is changing as companies are increasingly being held accountable, in their home countries, for the actions of the companies in their supply chains.

Social Economics

More recently, Thomas Piketty, the noted economist, has written extensively on the notion of profit. Piketty is a professor at the Ecole des Hautes Etudes en Science Sociales and the Paris School of Economics. He established an international reputation beyond the academic world with the publication of his major work, *Capital in the Twenty-first Century*. That book dealt in depth with the issue of inequality and the many problems it causes us. His more current *Brief History of Equality* picks up on most of the same themes as the first book but offers a somewhat more positive view. Piketty explains how much of human history has been one of responding to inequality, including various wars, migrations, the fight against slavery, and shifts in culture. Humans, he contends, tend to strive for equality and will take strong measures to achieve it.

In "The Rise of the Social Pillar," a paper published by CPA Canada, it was stated that "The scope of social matters is broad and includes human rights; diversity, equity and inclusion (DEI); relations with Indigenous peoples and communities; public health and safety; and privacy and freedoms."[2] The paper explored the social pillar of sustainability and provided direction to CPAs and other finance professionals as they navigate through the diverse range of social factors impacting organizations.

Another perspective on inequality is found in the work of Jude Wanniski, particularly in his book "The Way the World Works." It's often said that Wanniski formed the foundation for the economic theories of President Reagan. Most will remember that the central tenet of Reaganomics is that taxes should be cut and that the benefits will trickle down to the common people; a trickle-down approach to economic prosperity. Reagan recognized that cutting taxes could cause the country to run a deficit, which many felt to be unwise. However, his contention was that cutting taxes put more money into the hands of the people who would then spend and stimulate the economy, causing more economic activity and therefore more taxes. He felt there would be a good chance that the ultimate outcome would be higher-than-ever tax revenues for the government. It didn't appear to work as expected, however, because the national debt reached record highs after Reaganomics was implemented.

In addition, Western economies employ a graduated system of taxation, which means that tax cuts benefit the rich vastly more than the less fortunate segments of society, which contributes to inequality. And economic theory has clearly established that the rich spend a far smaller portion of their income on consumption and more on savings. As an example, the Truss government in the United Kingdom moved to cut taxes amid copious evidence that it would largely benefit the rich, then had to retreat from that policy because of loud protests from the public. In recent times, inequality has focused on the fact that 1 percent of the population holds the majority of wealth in the economy.

Measures to deal with diversity and discrimination also have had an effect on governance as well as operations, particularly in such areas as the selection of board members and occupants of the C-Suite. For example, among leading sustainability companies in the United States, 61 percent have implemented a sustainability committee at the board level. Tremendous pressure has been brought to bear on companies that have few or no female directors. Annual reports, as well as sustainability reports, must disclose this information.

As another example, in 2020, the U.S. Securities and Exchange Commission added human capital to its list of mandated disclosures in

10-K filings. This means that, as of 2021, publicly traded companies have been required to disclose any material information about their hiring practices, which can—depending on the company's business—include compensation costs, training methods, diversity numbers, and turnover rate.

While, as noted, sustainability information has been provided for some years in a separate report, this has not been adequate for meeting the new-found needs of investors, who want the information to be given to them in a manner more like financial information has been given. They want it to be consistent and reliable. They also are following investment indexes, such as the Dow Jones Sustainability Index, Bloomberg ESG Data Services, Thomson Reuters ESG Research Data, and others. The ESG scores measure companies' efforts in reducing carbon footprints, greener technology usage, community development projects, tax compliance, and avoidance of legal issues.

CHAPTER 3

The Historical Role of Profit

The apparent conflict felt by some people that paying attention to sustainability will hurt profits has been mentioned several times and is a widely held concern. But when you look into it, it is not only an unfounded concern; there is a widespread conclusion by many researchers that the opposite is true—paying attention to sustainability will enhance profits. Not paying attention to it will likely lessen profits, certainly in the longer term.

According to a recent study by Professor Witold Henisz of the Wharton School of Business, business leaders do not have to choose between their values and creating value. The study sets out the long-term business case for managers to pursue a wider purpose that contributes to societal goals.

"There's been a big debate about whether firms should maximize shareholder value or focus on a broader purpose, but those two aims are not necessarily in conflict. Managers don't have to choose between value and values,"* says Henisz, the vice dean and faculty director of Wharton's Sustainability Initiative.

He bases his conclusions on the link between a corporate purpose that emphasizes harmony among a wider set of stakeholders—customers, suppliers, communities, and government—and longer-term value creation. Such a link emphasizes long-term thinking. Also, these links lead stakeholders to contribute more to the firm's success because they buy into the strategies that relate to their own values. With more committed stakeholders and more long-term thinking, the company will be around for the longer term.

Professor Henisz also authored another paper that showed an investment portfolio containing a larger percentage of S&P 500 firms with

---

* https://knowledge.wharton.upenn.edu/article/the-long-term-business-case-for-corporate-purpose/.

higher broad stakeholder value versus shareholder value, and fewer companies with lower such ratios, substantially outperform benchmarks. Several other studies have shown similar results. Henisz adds that firms need to think about stakeholder relationships as an investment, instead of a cost to be managed because harmonizing varied stakeholder interests can take substantial time and effort.

That's because establishing a clear overall corporate purpose for a broad range of stakeholders should start with having an open dialogue with stakeholders. Henisz says, "Spend time talking to stakeholders and treat them as part of the value-creation process. Ask them about their goals and try to find some that overlap—this is your area of win-win." The objective is to find areas of interest to stakeholders that also are material to the value creation objectives of the company, including the financial well-being of the company. He says there's a boost to revenue growth and productivity when companies focus on issues that are relevant to stakeholders but also financially material to the firm.

Henisz adds that business leaders should focus less on stakeholders who are acting in their own self-interest, opportunistically, as this hampers progress toward wider goals. "For example, they might demand too good a deal, in which case the firm can cut them out and receive support from other stakeholders for doing so."

Many other thought leaders have taken the position that profits would be enhanced rather than harmed in the long term by attention to sustainability issues. The debate about the perceived conflict (or not) between profit and sustainability objectives will go on for some time to come. In thinking about this debate, it is worthwhile to stop and think about the purpose of profit in companies. It's not as simple as might at first be thought. The following look at history of profit explores this aspect of corporate purpose over the course of the history since Roman times.

If we ask the question—is profit the sole objective of a business?—the answer for most people will be that profit maximization is the main but not the sole objective of the business and that some reasonable level of profit is required in order to provide a livelihood for the owners, by providing a reasonable return on investment.

There's another view. In 2002, Professor Charles Handy of the United Kingdom wrote an article in the *Harvard Business Review*, in which he stated "The purpose of business is not to make a profit. It is to make a profit so that business can do something more or better."† In other words, profit is still a purpose of business, but it also is a means to an end.

A Brief History of Profits and Corporations

In his insightful and informative book *For Profit: A History of Corporations*,[1] William Magnuson traces the history of corporations and the role that profit has played in them over more than 2000 years. He begins with the Roman Republic prior to the advent of the Roman Empire. He feels that was when the idea of the corporation began, pointing out that "the term *corporation* derives from the Latin Word 'corpus' or body." Modern corporations can act as a single body in the law and offer some protection to their owners through the concept of limited liability. They also issue shares to shareholders and, through this means, can raise capital from the public. Corporations in Roman times didn't share all these attributes, but they did consist of groups of people acting as a body for business purposes.

The corporations in the Roman Republic were used to execute government contracts for activities such as road building and tax collecting. They also provided resources for the Roman army and indeed played a major role in building the most powerful army in the world at that time. Their objective was to provision the army, and raising capital and making profits was a means to that end.

The book went on to the time of the Italian Renaissance and the powerful Medici family. The Medicis built their fortune and remarkable status on their bank, which provided much funding for the armies of the state and the Pope. The Medici Bank generated new ideas about corporate structure. Rather than organizing itself as a single entity, located, managed, and owned in Florence, it set up an early multistructured form of holding company.

The Medici Bank in Florence was the principal entity, but other separate entities were formed across the continent. These separate branches had their own names, administrators and accounting

---

† https://hbr.org/2002/12/whats-a-business-for.

books—and had to report regularly to the bank holding company in Florence.[2]

With this structure, the Medicis were able to encourage the local managers, who were part owners of their own branches, to operate independently, within certain parameters, in the interests of the business. It also helped protect the corporation by spreading the risks across the entire corporate structure. Having offsite owners with managers running the company was to become a major feature of corporations after the Renaissance and, of course, into the present day.

The large trading companies of the 16th and 17th centuries in Britain added some new elements to corporate organization. One of these was the East India Company, formed in the year 1600, which led the way by being formed as a joint stock company.

Joint stock companies, a new concept in English law, proved particularly well suited to the grand voyages of the Age of Discovery. In short, they allowed businesses to sell stock in their companies to investors, who would pay in cash up front in return for a slice of future profits down the line.[3]

This approach worked well for those particular trading companies because they had high up-front costs preparing and manning their vessels and would only return profits, if any, several months or even years later. It took a long time to sail halfway around the world and back again in those days. The stockholders were very much venture capitalists. But the government of the day still played a very large role in their activities.

In those years, corporations could only be created by petitioning the crown. The East India Company was officially formed on New Year's Eve of 1600. There were 218 merchants involved and together they became "one Body Corporate and Politick, in Deed and in Name" with a monopoly over all trade between England and the East Indies (which covered anything east of the Cape of Good Hope).

The charter was clear that the purpose of the company was to contribute to the greatness of England in addition to the advancement of trade of merchandise and increased navigation. Profits would be necessary to sustain this trade.

While the company was spread around the Globe, it was actually run by a small group of men in a building in London. They soon learned that they required a system of management and controls to ensure that the managers in faraway places worked to the advantage of the overall business. This required a record-keeping system, which they adopted based on double-entry bookkeeping. Their systems were also used to maintain a record of the contents of warehouses and the terms of contracts.

The East India Company was one of the first companies to issue stock to their investors. The investors had limited liability, could trade their stocks, and were not involved in managing the company. Therefore, their prime interest was in the profitability of the company, which in turn led to a major change in the focus of management in that they now had to keep the investors happy, or else they might impair their ability to raise capital. The intention was that this reliable source of capital would enable the company to take a longer-term view of its prospects. In reality, the need to satisfy investors caused the company to take a short-term view, sometimes even leading to the falsification of profits.

The East India Company also maintained a military (shades of the Roman and Florentine versions), with eventually, by 1742, a force of some 1,200 soldiers at its base in Madras, India.

> While the East India Company would nominally continue its business for another seventy years (until the Indian Mutiny in 1857 led the British government to fully nationalize the company), its era as a private corporation was for the most part at an end. It had become an arm of the British government.[4]
>
> East India Company had—shown the power that corporations could wield in the world. The joint stock company and its progeny would come to dominate capitalism and commerce for the next several centuries. It would foster the colonization of the New World. It would usher in the Industrial Revolution. And it would fuel the spread and growth of the American economy.[5]

The need for companies to satisfy the investors' desire for higher stock prices led the companies to place an even greater emphasis on profits.

Fast forward to the 19th century and the formation of companies like the Union Pacific Railroad Company during the great westward migration. The Union Pacific was specifically formed to build a railroad from Iowa to California and meet up with another railroad started in California to be built by the Central Pacific Railroad Company. President Lincoln had decided that the railroad would be built by corporations. The companies were set up complete with capital stock and a board of directors. There was limited oversight by the government.

The result of this organization was that the stockholders stood to make lots of money on railroads, and they did. The incentive, opportunity, and limited oversight drove many of them to unethical practices, by owners who became known as the robber barons. They drove any competition out by various means including violence and kept costs down by importing cheap Chinese labor and exploiting its workers. Many fortunes were made in the railroads during this period. The country got its railroad, which provided the infrastructure to support the rapidly growing trade across the country in beef, grain, and other products.

The important transportation business took a major turn in the early 20th century when Henry Ford used the form of a corporation to make cars. They were not the first cars, but they were the first to be mass-produced and sold. The core of that mass production was the assembly line.

Using the productive power of the assembly line, the company developed a system of production of an unprecedented scale.

In 1913, Ford produced 68,733 Model Ts. In 1914, with the assembly line in full operation, the number rose to 170,211 units. Further refinements enabled the company in subsequent years to produce 200,000, then 300,000, and it went up after that. By 1918, Ford Motor Company was producing half of all U.S. automobiles: 700,000 cars per year.[6]

But there was another side to Henry Ford's reign over the automobile industry. Because it needed to sell all these cars being produced at a price people could afford, Ford created a working environment that proved draining and exhausting and often simply dehumanizing, mostly because of very long hours spent in bleak, repetitive work. "Outside the corporation, it created new appetites for consumption as an end in itself and, perhaps worse, incentives for corporations to generate those appetites on a societal scale. Mass production, it turned out, was a dangerous recipe for materialism, waste, and environmental destruction."[7]

The resulting controversy ultimately led to a very famous decision of the Michigan Supreme Court:

> A business corporation is organized and carried on primarily for the profit of the stockholders. The powers of the directors are to be employed for that end. The discretion of directors is to be exercised in the choice of means to attain that end, and does not extend to a change in the end itself, to the reduction of profits, or to the nondistribution of profits among stockholders in order to devote them to other purposes.[8]

Much of the corporate activity in the remaining years of the 20th century was consistent with this decision.

Around the same time, the famous economist and Nobel laureate Milton Friedman published a now infamous essay in which he proclaimed that the only responsibility of business firms is to increase their profits for the benefit of shareholders and that it should be the responsibility of governments to ensure societal welfare (Friedman 1970).[9]

There was more to come. The latter part of the 20th century saw the advent of multinational corporations. These companies no longer did business primarily in a single country and with a single domestic market. Instead, they operated wherever and whenever it made sense—regardless of jurisdictions or borders, currencies, or languages. Today, they are found everywhere, in companies like Walmart, Amazon, Apple, Exxon, and Facebook.

Multinationals really began with the big oil companies, when the world's use of oil grew dramatically in mid-century and local sources were not available. The companies began to explore and develop the resource wherever in the world it could be found. Eventually they settled largely in the Middle East. OPEC was formed to enable the oil-producing countries to help control the supply of oil, but it eventually led to the establishment of an embargo on the export of oil. After negotiations with OPEC failed, the big oil companies began to coordinate their shipments. This was organized by Exxon which was able to manage it because of its long history of global navigation—another indication of the power of the multinationals.

The multinational corporation represented an important shift in the nature of capitalism because the companies were freed from the clutches of their local governments. Since they operated so freely around the world, multinationals also drove the development of globalization.

In the years after World War II, national economies became increasingly interdependent as supply chains went global and people and ideas crossed borders as never before. International corporations encouraged these developments, not just by taking advantage of the economic prospects of cross-border trade but also by attracting the world's best and brightest and training them to succeed in the new world. A new kind of cosmopolitan capitalism began to take shape.

In retrospect, as Magnusson points out, "It should come as no surprise that the rise of the multinational in the post-World War II world coincided with the rise of the world's most pressing multinational problem: climate change."[10] Their efforts to seek out the most profitable jurisdictions in which to do business often meant finding countries that imposed lower taxes, fewer restrictions on employment conditions, or lax environmental rules.

Such behavior led some people to conclude that the modern corporation was no longer an exemplar of industry and efficiency but rather a symbol of greed and excess. To a degree, popular culture picked up on this view of corporations.

One of the most prominent practitioners of corporate takeovers during this period was Kohlberg, Kravis, and Roberts, generally known as KKR. They fostered the concept of the leveraged buyout (LBO) which meant they could buy a company with other investors' money and very little of their own. Then, they could sell it and make a huge profit on their own investment.

Another investor, Stephen Schwarzman, saw the tremendous potential of LBOs and formed the company Blackstone, now one of the world's largest investment companies, making Schwarzman a multibillionaire.

Perhaps the most striking recent example of the evolution of capitalism in the 20th and 21st centuries was the rise of the large multinational technology companies: companies like Facebook, Airbnb, Instagram,

Snapchat, X (formerly Twitter), and Uber. There are several others, all sharing a similar business model.

> No corporation in the history of the world has ever come anywhere close to the sheer size and scope of Meta (formerly Facebook). Not Standard Oil. Not the East India Company. Not the Medici Bank. Simply put, Facebook is unprecedented. In the evolution of the idea of the corporation, Facebook represents the apex predator.[11]

The U.S. election of 2016 witnessed a turnaround in that there grew a good deal of concern about "fake news" and misinformation carried by Facebook and other social media. In an appearance before Congress after the election of that year, Zuckerberg apologized for what his company had wrought.

> It's clear now that we didn't do enough to prevent these tools from being used for harm as well. That goes for fake news, foreign interference in elections, and hate speech, as well as developers and data privacy. We didn't take a broad enough view of our responsibility, and that was a big mistake. It was my mistake, and I'm sorry. I started Facebook, I run it, and I'm responsible for what happens here....

By most measures, Facebook has been supremely successful, but, much like the ancient Roman corporations had done during the 1st century BC, Facebook had ignored, dismissed, or simply didn't know how its behavior affected the common good, thus causing the government to make moves toward governing that behavior. This will plague all the big tech companies in the 21st century.

This leaves the question of what lessons can we learn from the history of corporations; in particular, what does their story tell us about the pressures for change facing modern corporations? And does it provide any hints about the possible future direction of the corporations?

Peter Drucker, one of the most popular management gurus of the 20th century, stated that a business which is mainly motivated by making money seldom grows well in the long run and never commands respect in society.[‡] His thinking has had an enormous impact on American and, ultimately, global thinking about companies. He also went on to say that businesses should earn profits but not ignore:

1. The provision of quality goods at reasonable prices to the consumers
2. Payment of all due taxes to the government treasury
3. Generating and offering good remuneration to its employees
4. Provision of hygienic working conditions
5. Contributing to the general welfare of the society[§]

Nevertheless, Drucker often stressed that businesses need to make money—and even lots of it. "No apology is needed for profit," Drucker wrote in his 1973 classic, *Management: Tasks, Responsibilities, Practices.*

Yet, at the same time, Drucker believed that all those dollars falling to the bottom line should ultimately help make for a stronger society. Specifically, Drucker wrote, "profit and profit alone can supply the capital . . . both for *more* jobs and for *better* jobs." Indeed, he declared, it is only with this purpose in mind that capitalism becomes "a moral system." It was a search for balance in corporate behavior and in society's view of the role of corporations.

Profits and Corporate Objectives

"Competent Boards"[¶] is an organization that offers online climate and sustainability programs that draw on the experience of more than 150 renowned board members, business leaders, and investors. Its faculty represents some of the world leaders in sustainability thinking and an emphasis on goals in addition to profit making for corporations. Hundreds of directors and senior executives have enrolled in these programs in order to transform their careers and their companies. An article posted

---

[‡] www.hrexchangenetwork.com/hr-talent-management/columns/the-purpose-of-business-is-not-to-make-a-profi.

[§] http://studylecturenotes.com/role-of-profit-in-business-is-profit-the-sole-objective-of-business/.

[¶] https://competentboards.com/.

to the Competent Boards' website summarizes the steps boards and management can pursue together to address these societal trends and become a force for good:

1. Adopt a social purpose as the reason your company exists and ensure it is implemented via the corporate strategy and in the company's relationships.
2. Set the course for your company to transform its business model and the ecosystem in which it operates to align with and contribute to a sustainable future.
3. Identify and collaborate with the influencers in your sector and value chain to address shared barriers and opportunities—this may include using the influence you hold in key industry and professional associations to mobilize them to adopt societal purposes.
4. Determine how your company can use its influence, reach, scale, platforms, and power to transition the systems in which it operates to be more sustainable and equitable.
5. Agree on a game plan for your business to become regenerative, restorative, socially just and a beacon of hope for your employees and partners.**

This review of the history of profits makes one conclusion particularly clear. Corporations have always had broad objectives beyond that of making money, but the making of profits is essential to the achievement of those objectives. In modern times, given the effects of extreme climate events and other social pressures on companies, a corporation's broad objectives must focus on sustainability, not necessarily exclusively, but in a major way.

** https://corostrandberg.com/do-you-know-the-role-of-your-business-in-society/.

CHAPTER 4

Sustainability Reporting and Investing

Sustainability Versus ESG Reporting

While the terms ESG reporting and sustainability reporting are often used interchangeably, strictly speaking, they are not the same. ESG refers to environmental, social, and governance and is therefore confined to these terms. Sustainability is a broader term, not necessarily confined to ESG and extending into other areas that might affect the sustainability of a company. While both ESG and sustainability are concerned with environmental, social, and governance factors, ESG focuses on evaluating the performance of companies based on these factors, while sustainability is a broader idea in that it also encompasses responsible and ethical business practices in a holistic manner.

The latest authoritative use of the term sustainability comes in the new standards issued by the International Sustainability Standards Board (ISSB). In ISSB Statement 1, the term sustainability-related financial disclosures is used. That term is defined as

> A particular form of general-purpose financial reports that provides an information about the reporting entity's sustainability related risks and opportunities that could reasonably be expected to affect the entity's cash flows, its access to finance or cost of capital over the short, medium or long term.

Since this definition refers to sustainability matters that would/could affect cash flow and other financial aspects of the organization, it is a subset of sustainability and ESG as generally understood.

There have been other definitions of sustainability disclosures which are all broad. Therefore, we conclude that sustainability is broader than ESG and shall use the terms accordingly.

Growth of Sustainability Reporting

During the late 80s, companies gradually began to report externally on their impacts on the environment and society. This voluntary reporting was partly in response to increasing demands from various nongovernmental organizations (NGOs) and investors for corporate accountability with regard to environmental and social impacts, and partly from companies that wished to portray themselves as good corporate citizens and protect their reputations in the wake of serious environmental incidents in certain industries.

Environmental Reporting

Environmental reporting, as a key component of sustainability reporting, covers the interaction of enterprises with the environment. This involves both the impact of enterprise activities on the environment (inside out) and the impact of the environment on company activities (outside in).

The environment has had a major, some would say outsized, impact on sustainability reporting. The interest in and need for environmental reporting has been accelerated by the devastating effects environmental issues have had (or will have) on business profitability and the performance of investment portfolios. People have become more aware that the types of events that have happened do indeed have serious financial implications. Moreover, the social consciousness of investors generally has risen in recent years, leading to a greater interest in environmental issues and what companies can do about them. Finally, organizations such as the SEC and the EU have released sustainability disclosure requirements. For example, the Securities and Exchange Commission (SEC) stated that

> Investors need information about climate-related risks—and it is squarely within the Commission's authority to require such disclosure in the public interest and for the protection of investors—because climate-related risks have presented financial consequences that investors in public companies consider in making investment and voting decisions.*

---

* www.sec.gov/files/rules/proposed/2022/33-11042.pdf.

Companies have responded to this increasing investor awareness by releasing growing numbers of sustainability reports. However, this has often been a superficial response, replete with greenwashing. More substantively, some companies have also placed more emphasis on the role of sustainability factors in their ongoing strategic development and management processes.

Companies Reporting on the Environment

A 2022 report *Getting to Net Zero* from the International Federation of Accountants (IFAC) included the following findings:

- 66 percent of the large, exchange-traded companies that IFAC reviewed included some type of emissions reduction target in their corporate disclosures.
- These emissions targets used a variety of terminology and only 39 percent incorporated Scope 3 emissions.
- Most companies (90 percent) who disclose emissions targets also provide a disclosure about how they plan to reach their target.
- Only 24 percent of companies with a plan include some past expenditure or future estimate of expenditures to implement plan actions.

EcoAct, an international climate consultancy and project developer, performs studies every year of companies reporting on climate. In their report on 2022, they highlighted three companies from a list of the top 10 companies worldwide.[†]
The three were Telefónica, Sanofi, and E.ON.

Telefónica

An IBEX-listed telecommunications company, Telefónica, is committed to net zero by 2040 with a target to reduce emissions by 90 percent. It

---

[†] *The 2022 Corporate Climate Reporting Performance Report, EcoAct.*

has a clear strategy for offsetting the residual 10 percent following best-practice criteria, focusing on environmental and social cobenefits. It also has a clear action plan demonstrating a credible 1.5°C-aligned transition plan for its business and is delivering emissions reductions.

Sanofi

French multinational pharmaceutical and health care company Sanofi has ranked second highest this year. The company acknowledges that climate change is perhaps the greatest challenge of our age. It has aligned itself with the new SBTi Net-Zero Standard with validated near-term targets across all scopes and pending validation of its long-term targets. To achieve its goal, it is focusing on a range of actions, including engaging with its suppliers, internal carbon pricing, installing solar panels, and driving positive change within its sector through innovations such as its Evolution Vaccine Facilities (EVF). It also achieved emissions reductions aligned to a 1.5°C trajectory.

E.ON

An electric utility company based in Germany with more than 51 million customers across Europe has SBTi-verified 1.5°C-aligned near-term targets to reduce Scope 1 and 2 emissions by 75 percent and Scope 3 emissions by roughly 50 percent (including 42% use of sold products) by 2030. It aims for a 100 percent reduction across all scopes by 2050, and progress toward these targets is factored into the management board's compensation. The company has also pledged to invest €27 billion between 2022 and 2026 in the energy transition via the expansion of renewable energy networks and to offer new services to its customers over the same timescale. E.ON achieved emissions reductions across all scopes in the past year.

Social Reporting

While sustainability reporting has always included the environmental, social, and governmental elements of reporting, much attention has been given to the environmental element. However, the social and governmental areas are important and still draw attention from stakeholders, particularly in reference to matters around diversity and equality. Consumers, among other stakeholders, look to sustainability reports to determine if their dollars are supporting a company whose values align with theirs.

Social reporting covers social issues like a company's labor practices, talent management, product safety, and data security. Lack of proper data security, for example, has caused some companies considerable embarrassment and money, especially when customer data is compromised.

Labor Practices

Treatment of labor is a major factor in the field of sustainability. Issues like fair pay, equality, and diversity are top of mind for many people. Also of particular interest to many is the question of the treatment of minorities, particularly in foreign countries where some companies can be found using child labor or even slavery. This is unacceptable behavior.

Cybersecurity

"Almost two-thirds of the world's institutional investors are concerned about the impact of cyber security threats on their investments, making it investors' foremost environmental, social and governance (ESG) risk," according to the 2019 RBC Global Asset Management Responsible Investment Survey.

Astra's prediction is that eight trillion dollars will be lost to *cybercrimes* by the end of 2023, which is almost a third of the U.S. GDP in 2022 and twice as much as India's predicted GDP in March 2023. The global loss to cybercrime will grow more than 15 percent year by year to reach $10.5 trillion by 2025.

Companies are struggling hard to deal with this issue, but the growing sophistication of the operators along with the complexity of modern systems is making it very difficult. Consequently, organizations around the world spent around U.S. $150 billion in 2021 on cybersecurity, representing annual growth of 12.4 percent.[1] Most experts feel this level of spending is not sufficient in the face of the enormous threat faced by most companies.

Cybersecurity and cybercrime are major specialties of considerable complexity. Much has been written about them and a full discussion of them is well beyond the scope of this book.

Governance Reporting

Governance reporting covers matters like board diversity, executive pay, and business ethics. Companies often have a governance committee of the board of directors to monitor governance policy and procedures. The tradition in the past for many companies has been to issue a separate report on governance. However, the more recent treatment has been to include it in their sustainability report, except that some specific disclosures are required by the regulators to be included with or in the financial statements.

Standards for Sustainability Reporting

Global Reporting Initiative Standards

The move toward standards for ESG or sustainability disclosures was led by the Global Reporting Initiative (GRI), which was founded in Boston in 1997 following the environmental damage of the Exxon Valdez oil spill, eight years previously. Their goal was to create the first accountability mechanism to ensure companies adhere to responsible environmental conduct principles, which afterward was broadened to include social, economic, and governance issues.

The first version of the GRI guidelines was published in 2000—providing the first global framework for sustainability reporting. A year later, GRI was established as an independent, nonprofit institution. In 2002, the GRI's Secretariat relocated to Amsterdam in The Netherlands. As demand for, and uptake of, the GRI guidelines steadily grew, the guidelines continued to be expanded and improved.

As sustainability reporting spread around the world, GRI began opening regional offices in Brazil (2007), China (2009), India (2010), the United States (2011), South Africa (2013), Colombia (2014), and Singapore (2019). Several GRI global conferences were held during this period, and since then, they have held regular regional or virtual events and summits.

In 2016, GRI transitioned from providing guidelines to setting the first global standards for sustainability reporting—the GRI standards.

The standards are developed with multistakeholder contributions and are rooted in the public interest. The GRI sustainability reporting standards are the first and to date the most widely adopted global standards for sustainability reporting. These evolved over the years and were widely adopted by large companies around the world, becoming the de facto standard for sustainability reporting.

As the GRI announced at the time,

> The GRI Standards enable organizations to report information about the most significant impacts of their activities and business relationships on the economy, environment, and people, including impacts on their human rights. Such impacts are of primary importance to sustainable development and to organizations' stakeholders, and they are the focus of sustainability reporting.[2]

The GRI standards are classified into three series. First are the universal standards, which are intended to be followed by all companies. Then there is the sector series, which are intended to be followed by companies operating in the designated sectors. Finally, there is the topics series of standards, which companies use according to the particular material topics on which they must report.

The GRI Universal Standards

The first universal standard, GRI 1, introduces the purpose and system of the standards and explains the key concepts of sustainability reporting. It also specifies the requirements and reporting principles to be followed.

The second universal standard, GRI 2, covers disclosures about an organization's reporting practices and other organizational details, such as its activities, governance, and policies. This information provides insight into the profile and scale of the organization and offers a context for understanding the organization's impact on the environment and the impact of the environment on it.

The third universal standard, GRI 3, gives step-by-step guidance on how to determine material topics. As such, the standard provides disclosures about the organization's process of determining and managing its material topics.

With the inclusion of the sector and topics standards, the GRI has released the most comprehensive set of sustainability standards so far, including, for example, standards on labor/management relations, occupational health and safety, training and education, diversity and equal opportunity, and nondiscrimination, among others.

These are important issues, and many of them relate to the issue of inequality. Inequality is at the root of most major social upheavals in history, as well as the social unrest currently evident in several countries around the world. Inequality needs to be addressed by everyone, including individuals, governments, and companies.

Sustainability Accounting Standards Board

In 2011, the Sustainability Accounting Standards Board (SASB) was formed and began issuing standards. However, there was a significant difference from GRI in that these standards were directed to ESG issues relevant to financial performance. As SASB put it, "the Standards identify the subset of environmental, social, and governance issues most relevant to financial performance in each industry."[‡] This idea was carried forward by the ISSB.

The SASB was a progeny of the SASB Foundation, a nonprofit organization set up by a group of prominent businesses and individuals in the United States to help businesses around the world "identify, manage and report on the sustainability topics that matter most to their investors." SASB standards differ by industry, enabling investors and companies to compare performance from company to company within an industry and are developed based on extensive feedback from companies, investors, and other market participants as part of a transparent, publicly documented

---

[‡] Standards Overview, SASB.

process. Compliance with SASB pronouncements has increased in recent years, driven in part by the demands of stakeholders who recognize the tremendous financial impact of environmental disasters and issues.

By 2016, after five years of working with investors, companies, and other experts, SASB had issued standards for use by companies in over 70 industry sectors in order to enhance the comparability and usefulness of sustainability disclosures. In 2022, responsibility for the SASB standards was assumed by the ISSB operating under the umbrella of the IFRS Foundation.

Task Force on Climate-Related Financial Disclosures

Because of the perceived threat of climate change to the stability of worldwide financial systems and institutions, the Financial Stability Board (FSB) under Mark Carney (former governor of the Bank of Canada and the Bank of England) created the international Task Force on Climate-Related Financial Disclosures (TCFD) to meet investor information needs. In 2017, the TCFD released its recommendations for disclosures by financial institutions and companies about governance, strategy, risk (physical, liability, and transition-related), metrics, and targets.

As the FSB TCFD, the TCFD develops voluntary, consistent, climate-related financial risk disclosures for use by companies in providing information to investors, lenders, insurers, and other stakeholders. The task force considers the physical, liability, and transition risks associated with climate change and what constitutes effective financial disclosures across industries. Pressure is mounting in all major economies and jurisdictions to adopt, implement, and enforce TCFD-specified climate disclosures as a core element of information needed by responsible investors. TCFD recommendations are widely respected and followed and were required by some regulators, such as the SEC in the United States.

International Sustainability Standards Board

The ISSB issued its first two standards in June 2023. They were IFRS S1 (*General requirements for disclosure of sustainability-related financial information*) and IFRS S2 (*Climate-related disclosures*). They specifically mention compliance with the recommendations of the TCFD and are likely to be the predominant standards for sustainability reporting in the coming years. The ISSB standards also incorporate the SASB standards by reference.

While S1 covers general standards, S2 covers sustainability standards relating to the climate-related risks and opportunities faced by the organization that would have an influence on financial results. They have set out the standards related to some of the risks and opportunities that might be covered but mention the GRI standards for reference in areas not yet covered by ISSB standards. The ISSB standards are intended to conform to the qualitative characteristics as set out in the conceptual framework included in the IFRS standards, which provides them some consistency with financial accounting standards and, therefore, more suitability for inclusion in financial reports.

NASDAQ

A committee report on sustainability reporting published by NASDAQ identified three reasons why companies should begin reporting ESG information. These include the following:

1. Global regulatory policy shifts—Many regulatory bodies have been calling for companies to provide such disclosures. For example, the U.S. SEC added, in 2020, human capital to its list of mandated disclosures in 10-K filings. Starting in 2022, European investors are required to comply with the new EU Taxonomy under which investors must disclose how much of their investment activity can be classified as sustainable, which in turn forces companies to disclose certain "green" revenue or capital expenditure metrics.

2. Lack of trust in ESG data not based on reliable sources—The lack of trust is in data that do not originate with the companies or data that are disclosed by the companies but without knowledge of its sources. The thought here is that data reported by the company are likely to be more trustworthy, especially if there are standards to encourage consistency and assurance provided on it.

3. Strong investor interest in ESG—Investors have not been waiting for companies to disclose their sustainability data but rather

have been hiring ESG analysts to dig out the data and evaluate its reliability. Latest data from NASDAQ research shows that of the 150 top investment managers, each has an average of eight analysts. It's a burgeoning industry!

As a minimum, these are good reasons to pay more attention to sustainability issues.

After the ISSB standards were issued, there was confusion about how they fitted with the GRI standards. Consequently, the GRI issued an additional explanation in their GRI 1 in a separate box in that standard, which explained that the GRI standards enabled organizations to report information about the most significant impacts of their activities and business relationships on the economy, environment, and people, including impacts on their human rights. Such impacts are of importance to sustainable development and an organization's stakeholders, such as investors, workers, customers, or local communities.

On the other hand, the ISSB disclosure standards require disclosing material information about all sustainability-related risks and opportunities that could reasonably be expected to affect an organization's business model or strategy and consequently its cash flows, access to finance, or cost of capital over the short, medium, or long term. Thus, the ISSB standards are of greatest interest to investors. The GRI went on to explain that the use of the GRI standards and the ISSB disclosure standards together provide a comprehensive overview of an organization's sustainability-related impacts, risks, and opportunities. The GRI concludes that the perspectives that each of these standards bring are relevant in their own right and complement each other. In 2022, the GRI and ISSB signed a memorandum of understanding to coordinate their work.

Proposal of the Securities and Exchange Commission

On March 21, 2022, the SEC introduced a proposal for climate-related disclosures that would require public companies to make such disclosures largely in line with the TCFD, especially in its emphasis on the risks involved and ISSB requirements. The proposal suggested enhancements to existing disclosures already made by some corporations.

One notable aspect of the SEC proposal was the requirement for companies to separate and disclose the impact of physical risks, transition risks, and other identified climate-related risks on their financial statements. This includes reflecting the effects of events, like severe storms on revenue, assets, and liabilities, along with contextual information about how those measures were derived. Additionally, companies would need to disclose details about the properties and operations exposed to such risks, promoting transparency.

The proposal also responds to calls for an independent check on greenhouse gas (GHG) emissions disclosures. It mandates separate disclosure of Scope 1 and 2 GHG emissions, subjecting them to limited assurance by an independent party one year after compliance with the rule. After two additional fiscal years, a more thorough independent review called reasonable assurance would be required. Independent reviews help reduce conflicts of interest, enhance data quality, and increase reliability.

The text emphasizes the need for robust accountability in emissions disclosures and encourages careful consideration of the scope of such disclosures. Investors recognize the materiality and necessity of GHG emissions disclosures in their decision-making process, underscoring the importance of accuracy, comparability, and reliability. A strong gatekeeping function is vital to ensure the integrity of disclosed information.

Furthermore, the proposal addresses the challenge posed by net-zero pledges made by companies. It asserts that without specific, standardized, and reliable disclosures, it is difficult to assess and measure the progress made toward achieving these pledges. Companies must disclose their Scope 3 emissions (indirect emissions through their value chain) if they include them in a GHG reduction target. The proposal also requires disclosure on the use of carbon offsets, including the amount of carbon reduction represented by the offset and information about its source. This ensures transparency about the means used to arrive at a company's net emissions disclosure measure.

Overall, the proposal aims to provide investors with meaningful and calibrated disclosures, and feedback is encouraged to ensure the information keeps pace with market expectations.

Scope 1 emissions are direct emissions from sources that are owned or controlled by an organization. Examples of would-be emissions from on-site fossil fuel combustion include process emissions and those from industrial processes, refrigeration, heating, air conditioning, electricity generation, and emissions from company-owned vehicles.

Scope 2 emissions are indirect emissions from the consumption of purchased energy, like electricity and heat. These emissions are not directly controlled by the company, but rather, are a result of its activities and can be influenced by purchasing decisions. For example, if a company purchases electricity from a power plant that generates electricity from coal, the emissions from the power plant are considered Scope 2 emissions for the company.

Scope 3 emissions are all other indirect emissions that are a result of the activities of an organization but are not included in Scope 2. Examples include emissions from employee commuting and business travel, waste disposal, and the use of purchased goods and services throughout an organization's supply chain.

European Union Standards (EFRAG and CSRD)

The European Commission (EC) announced in 2020 that the European Financial Reporting Advisory Group (EFRAG) was to develop recommendations for nonfinancial reporting standards, although the decision to mandate standards lies with the European Council.

> EFRAG will mobilise a balanced and broad task force, taking into account a wide range of stakeholders and expertise, to prepare technical advice. The recommendations must build on existing standards and frameworks, and will be developed in close association with existing standard setting organisations.

The European Union (EU) issued their corporate sustainability reporting directive (CSRD) in January 2023 that requires large companies to publish regular reports on the social and environmental impacts of their activities, beginning with financial periods ending in 2024 and published in 2025. It will replace the previous nonfinancial reporting directive issued in 2014.

The CSRD goes beyond the standards of S1 of the ISSB and the requirements of the SEC, both of which only require the disclosure of sustainability events that have or are likely to have an impact on cash flows and financial position. The CSRD calls for disclosure of information on sustainability (climate and other matters) that is likely to have a significant impact on the company and others. Like the SEC, the CSRD also requires assurance on the sustainability information that companies report and will provide for the use of a digital taxonomy to disclose the information in digital form.

At this time, the CSRD carries forward details of the previous EU directive on sustainability of 2014 which called for consideration of other pre-existing standards, including ISO 26000 and the GRI standards.

To implement the principles of the CSRD, which is a directive and not a set of standards, EFRAG began publishing the European Sustainability Reporting Standards (ESRS). In April 2023, EFRAG and GRI published a joint statement on the high level of interoperability achieved between the ESRS and the GRI standards.

> Following the requirement of the CSRD to—take account of existing standards, ESRS and GRI definitions, concepts and disclosures regarding impacts are fully or, when full alignment was not possible due to the content of the CSRD mandate, closely aligned.

These developments will encourage existing companies using GRI standards to report under the ESRS standards. Entities reporting under ESRS are considered to be reporting with reference to the GRI standards and will therefore avoid the burden of multiple reporting.

Canadian Securities Administrators' Guidelines

The Canadian Securities Administrators (CSA) and Ontario Securities Commission (OSC) in Canada have also released guidelines for climate-related disclosure. On August 1, 2019, the CSA issued *CSA Staff*

Notice 51-358: Reporting of Climate Change-Related Risks that provides guidance on risk identification and disclosure by reporting issuers as it relates to climate change.

Commonalities in the Disclosure Initiatives

All of these initiatives and standards have two things in common:

1. Their need for and dependence on a very wide variety of data types and enormous quantities of data, plus the technologies for both companies and report/data users to handle the data.
2. The opportunity for reporting companies to use Internet and website technologies (including data tagging such as XBRL) effectively for presenting information and making it accessible, comparable, and "friendly" to users.

Because of these commonalities, information technology is an essential enabler today for both providers and users of sustainability reporting.

Adequacy of the Standards

According to GRI, sustainability reporting is now a common practice among upward of 5,000 of the world's largest companies, and two-thirds of these companies are reporting in line with the GRI standards.

Moving toward data-centric digital reporting would help companies respond more easily to information requests from data users, reduce the inaccuracies of data mining from PDF reports, and address the growing demand for sustainability information from stock exchanges, governments, investors, and consumers.

Materiality

A significant effect of the new standards was that, since they are pertinent to financial performance, the concept of materiality assumed a new importance since materiality is such an important element of financial disclosure. The question is how would materiality be measured when dealing with such matters as storms and environmental degradation.

The ISSB standards discuss materiality and provide a definition as follows:

> In the context of sustainability-related financial disclosures, information is material if omitting, misstating or obscuring that information could reasonably be expected to influence decisions that primary users of "general purpose" financial reports make on the basis of those reports, which include financial statements and sustainability-related financial disclosures and which provide information about a specific reporting entity.

This definition is consistent with the definition usually associated with financial reporting.

The GRI also discusses materiality in its standards but takes care to differentiate between two types of materiality. One of these is financial materiality, which is defined in the same way as ISSB materiality. But the GRI also defines "impact materiality," which is a measure of the importance of sustainability items or events to all organization's stakeholders, such as investors, workers, customers, or local communities. Impact materiality was also adopted in the ESRS as one of the two dimensions (impact materiality and financial materiality) on which an organization needs to report.

While financial materiality is determined by the effect an event or item has on the finances of the company, impact materiality reflects the impact of the company on the world. For example, an initiative to support a local community baseball team would not likely be reported by a large organization (although it might be reported to the local community), while a decision to switch from gas-powered trucks to electric trucks could well be considered material enough to report to all the stakeholders.

Both financial materiality and impact materiality together are known as double materiality, which can be taken together in making disclosure decisions. Measuring both types of materiality involves the exercise of judgment in various degrees. Generally, though, impact materiality involves a greater exercise of judgment because of an absence of established benchmarks to aid in the judgment. Double materiality is also included in the EU/EFRAG/CSRD standards.

The strong need for judgment in making materiality decisions will continue to plague sustainability reporting and we can expect more guidance and standards to be forthcoming to address this issue.

Hope for Less Greenwashing

Generally, sustainability reports have been provided as separate narrative-style reports with some key performance indicators included. So far, too much of the sustainability reporting that has been provided has varied widely among companies in terms of quality, content, and reliability, which has led to accusations of greenwashing (disinformation disseminated by an organization so as to present an environmentally responsible public image). The hope is that the new standards will help to remedy this quality issue.

Confusion Caused by Plethora of Standards and Standards-Setting Bodies

One result of the new ISSB (as well as SASB) standards was that they in effect redefined the term sustainability standards because they referred to their standards as such, but as they said, in fact only covered a subset of sustainability standards as previously understood, that is, those related to financial performance. This has been confusing to many people. The plethora of standards-setting bodies in the sustainability area has added to the confusion. This is being addressed by having responsibility for most of the standard setting for sustainability reporting assumed under the umbrella of the IFRS Foundation. However, considerable confusion remains because all of the different standards still exist separately.

It was not until the early 2000s, however, that the mainstream investment community, especially major public pension funds, began to consider that E, S, and G factors could materially affect a company's financial performance and future value to investors and indeed be material for sound investment decision making. As firm empirical evidence grew, with strong academic backing, demand exploded for ESG-type data that investors and analysts could use in planning and evaluating investment portfolios.

Sustainability reports proved inadequate as sources for this data because their disclosures were designed to meet the broad information needs of stakeholders in general, not to present or highlight information material to investors. In 2005, the UN Global Compact coined the acronym ESG, and in 2006, the UN Principles of Responsible Investment organization was founded to promote institutional investment practices built on the integration of E, S, and G factors into the investment policies and decision making of signatory investment institutions.

ESG reporting continued to evolve and grow to meet the expectations of its broader audiences. A whole new data-driven industry thus emerged to fuel investors' ESG information needs, including ratings, data research, and aggregation, such as Bloomberg terminals with downloadable data and spreadsheets for analysts.

ESG Investing

Sometimes referred to as responsible investing or as socially responsible investing (SRI), ESG investing has become a major force in the investment community because of popular demand that companies show some concern about environmental, social, and governance issues.

More recently, responsible investing has moved closer to the mainstream, with stakeholders demanding companies act more responsibly in their environmental and social impacts. This has been a driving factor for corporate change. Since investors are interested in information on ESG matters, they have been demanding more and better information in order to make decisions. This growing trend is being driven by Millennials and others who want to align their investments with their personal values.

Investopedia defines SRI as involving "investing in companies that promote ethical and socially conscious themes including environmental sustainability, social justice, and corporate ethics, in addition to fighting against gender and sexual discrimination."

An article in the Harvard Business Review (April 2022) titled "ESG Investing Isn't Designed to Save the World" addressed the issue that people assume ESG investing is designed to reward companies that are helping the planet. In fact, ESG ratings which underlie ESG fund selection are based on the impact of the changing world on company profits. Asset management firms have been happy to let the confusion go uncorrected since ESG funds are highly popular and come with higher management fees.

So, how does a responsible investor proceed in the face of this conundrum? There are several ways:

1. Invest in companies that are most likely to have a small environmental footprint. They might feel that strip mining companies, for example, don't meet the definition, but that banks do.
2. Invest in funds specifically designed to hold green companies. Examples of such funds are iShares ESG Aware MSCI USA ETF (ESGU), iShares MSCI USA SRI UCITS ETF (SUAS), and iShares ESG Aware MSCI EAFE ETF (ESGD). iShares is a Blackrock company.
3. Invest in companies that specifically work in green areas, like recycling and power generation, organic groceries, and sustainable fisheries. Technology is often a popular area for SRI investing. Top SRI investments are Microsoft (MSFT), Alphabet GOOG, Nvidia (NVDA), and Tesla (TSLA). Other top green investments include Visa (V), Procter & Gamble (PG), Home Depot (HD), AbbVie (ABBV), and MasterCard (MA).
4. Invest in GICs that are market-linked to ESG investments.

SRI investing has become a popular area of investing, and most major financial institutions such as Royal Bank of Canada, Morgan Stanley, and Citigroup now offer products that specialize in this area.

A number of organizations also provide ESG Risk Ratings and statistics. These include, among others, MSCI, Morningstar, Sustainalytics, and Investopedia. These ratings measure a company's management of financially relevant ESG risks and opportunities by assigning a quantitative metric, such as a numerical score or letter rating, to the ESG efforts undertaken by a company or organization.

For example, MSCI analyzes the risks and opportunities faced by a company and assigns a percentage to that company, reflecting the scale of its efforts in this area. It then places the result into one of its rating categories which is a range of CCC, B, BB, BBB, A, AA, and AAA.

Investors can use these ratings to help them choose investments, particularly if they employ responsible investing in their decisions. Interest in responsible investing has increased in Europe and decreased in the United States over recent years. Nevertheless, with the increased disclosures called for by regulators and standards-setting boards, it will remain on the radar for investors. "However, there is an issue in that ratings agency processes are a black box and users have no way of really comparing; it is a false sense of comparability and transparency."

Should Sustainability Reporting Do More?

There are a great many companies around the world reporting on sustainability because of the widespread recognition of the importance of ESG. This recognition has led to the view that sustainability reporting may not be going far enough and that there needs to be greater recognition in corporate reporting that sustainability and financial considerations are closely related and intertwined.

In the next chapter, we will examine the evolution of integrated reporting to connect sustainability information with financial information and intangibles to provide a holistic view of how companies create value for stakeholders, including investors, and the essential roles of the Internet and company websites as well as data collection and management technologies in this process.

CHAPTER 5

From Sustainability Reporting to Integrated Thinking

The focus on reporting to shareholders discussed in the previous chapter led at least in part to the idea of integrated reporting, which would involve bringing together financial and sustainability reporting in a single report. That happened because financial results have always been reported primarily to shareholders, and if sustainability is to be reported to shareholders, it makes sense to bring those reports together. It makes even more sense to integrate them to reduce duplication and add meaning to the events being reported upon.

An integrated report is defined in the Integrated Reporting Framework as[*]: "A concise communication about how an organization's strategy, governance, performance and prospects, in the context of its external environment, lead to the creation, preservation or erosion of value in the short, medium and long term."[1] The key here is the phrase "the creation, preservation or erosion of value." The focus of value creation is on the six capitals (under their definition) that organizations employ to provide a foundation for their business:

1. Financial capital, represented by financial assets
2. Manufactured capital, represented by infrastructure, buildings, and so on
3. Intellectual capital, represented by the knowledge base of the organization

---

[*] A publication of the IFRS Foundation, available at www.integratedreporting.org/resource/international-ir-framework/.

4. Human capital, consisting of human resources
5. Social and relationship capital, including all the relationships of the company with its stakeholders
6. Natural capital, represented by the environmental elements such as land, water, and air.

In integrated reporting, the success or otherwise of the organization is measured by how it has added to or detracted from the value of these capitals. Clearly, therefore, the measure of success extends far beyond the traditional financial measures. And the fact that all of these capitals are discussed in the same integrated report means their interrelationships would be taken into account. So, the various capitals need to be considered as an interrelated group and presented in that way, rather than simply being included as separate items in the same report.

Professional Guidance and Standards

Guidance for the preparation of integrated reports initially came from the International Integrated Reporting Council (IIRC), which was formed in 2010 when the Global Reporting Initiative joined forces with Accounting for Sustainability, a UK charity sponsored by (then) Prince Charles in order to advance integrated reporting worldwide as a mainstream reporting practice and to develop a framework to guide companies in producing integrated reports.

The IIRC was a global coalition of regulators, investors, companies, standard setters, the accounting profession, academia, and nonprofit organizations that are independent of governments (NGOs). After issuing a discussion paper in 2011, and a consultation draft early in 2013, the IIRC[†] released its international framework for integrated reporting in December 2013. The IIRC and its Integrated Reporting Framework were transferred to the IFRS Foundation in August 2022. The IASB (International Accounting Standards Board) and ISSB (International Sustainability Standards Board) are encouraging businesses to continue using the framework.

[†] https://integratedreporting.org/the-iirc-2/.

The advent of integrated reporting does not mean that financial statements and sustainability reports will suddenly become obsolete. On the contrary, shareholders and investors will certainly continue to expect and need financial statements, along with an MD&A (Management Discussion and Analysis) Commentary and the other normal accoutrements of financial and business reporting; many types of stakeholders will certainly continue to seek the more detailed sustainability information they receive in sustainability reports; while institutional investors, fund managers, and analysts will expect material sustainability disclosures and TCFD (Task Force on Climate-Related Financial Disclosures)-based climate disclosures that may not be included in a concise integrated report. This may be transitional since it is possible that eventually integrated reporting, as it matures, could replace traditional reports, but that won't happen overnight.

Integrated reporting aims to address the limitations of traditional financial reporting by providing a comprehensive picture of an organization's performance, risks, opportunities, and the broader context in which it operates. As an example, suppose there has been a fire at one of the manufacturing plants and all materials used for manufacturing have been destroyed. The materials included paint and chemicals that emitted toxic fumes into the atmosphere. As a result, nearby residents had to evacuate for several days. The financial loss of this fire would be disclosed along with the environmental implications in terms of the resultant pollution and how it was dealt with. In addition, the social implications might include the extent and nature of the disruption to the community that ensued, as well as the actions taken to remedy this for the residents. Finally, the governance implications might include a review of any governance failings that might have led to the fire as well as any remedial action taken, such as regular inspections by fire marshals or amendments to the governance structure as it applies to fire safety. In other words, readers of the report would gain an understanding of all the implications of the event in one place.

The integration concept would extend to other aspects of the company's activities. At the strategic level, the company might have adopted a policy of sourcing materials from other countries in distant lands, such as South America and Africa, thus extending its supply chain to those countries. Cultural and political differences might mean that the goods to be procured are produced under conditions that would not meet the approval of stakeholders and might be at the expense of human rights. For example, the cloth being purchased might be produced by children without pay, effectively constituting forced child labor. That would mean the company needs to adopt policies and procedures that protect against being caught up in supporting that behavior, like ID checks, funding education for children in local communities, fair pay, and so on. In an integrated report, they would disclose the policies they have adopted to conduct due diligence procedures on their extended supply chain, both at inception and over the coming years. They would also actually activate these policies and take any remedial action that might be required.

Other ideas somewhat similar to integrated reporting have gained some attention over the years. For example, triple bottom line reporting is a business concept that says firms should commit to measuring their social and environmental impact as well as their financial performance. It posits that, rather than focusing only on generating profit, or the standard "bottom line," this be presented in terms of three P's—Profit, People, and the Planet. It is another way of reporting on financial, social, and environmental matters together. The triple bottom line idea has won some attention among theoreticians but presents some severe practical challenges. It supposes that the people and planet results can be measured in some way comparable to the profit measurements. However, there have been centuries of standards and practical experience behind the profit measures, and no such parallel exists for the people and planet measures. The measures that are evolving in sustainability and integrated reporting consist of specific metrics that often have no counterpart in financial reporting. Of course, this does not invalidate the concept; it just renders it less likely to be adopted as quickly as other means of achieving the desired reporting goals, such as integrated reporting.

Triple bottom line reporting has, however, been used in some cases. In a report issued by the Danish company, Novozymes, the company used GRI's G2 guidelines as a basis for its triple bottom line reporting. While the report is sometimes credited with being the first integrated report, it is clear, however, that the report was more combined than integrated since there was little discussion of the interrelationships of the various components in the report.

Some companies would inevitably lead the way in experimenting with integrated reporting, by including in their annual reports and websites, information about those aspects of their environmental and social performance, policies and targets, which they saw as fundamentally linked to their overall business and performance, financial results, and prospects for future value creation.

Presenting these financial and nonfinancial types of information together, connected in one report, would, they believed, be more effective in communication with stakeholders than just separate, stand-alone sustainability reports and would also, like a good MD&A, help investors and analysts understand with greater insight the context for and broad spectrum of value drivers behind a company's reported financial results and future prospects. The stage was set for wider experimentation and development of what we now call integrated reporting. Ultimately, the following principles emerged.

Principles of Integrated Reporting

- *Strategic Focus and Future Orientation*: Integrated reports go beyond historical financial data and emphasize an organization's strategy for long-term value creation. This enables stakeholders to understand how an organization is positioning itself for the future and responding to changing circumstances.
- *Connectivity of Information*: The interconnectedness of various aspects of an organization's operations is highlighted in integrated reports. For example, a company's environmental practices may affect its reputation, which in turn could influence customer loyalty and financial performance.
- *Stakeholder Relationships*: Integrated reporting acknowledges the influence of different stakeholder groups on an organization's success. By identifying and addressing these stakeholders, organizations demonstrate a commitment to effective engagement and responsible decision making.

- *Materiality*: Integrated reports focus on material matters—those that have a significant impact on the organization's ability to create value and are likely to influence investment decisions. This helps avoid information overload and ensures that only relevant data are presented.
- *Conciseness, Consistency, and Reliability*: Reports are designed to be clear, concise, and easily understandable. They also maintain consistency across different sections and reporting periods, allowing stakeholders to compare performance over time.
- *Credibility and Reliability*: Integrated reports are built on robust data collection processes, ensuring the reliability of information. Transparency about data sources, methodologies, and governance practices enhances credibility.

Examples of Integrated Reports

Following are some examples of integrated reports (available on the respective company's websites):

Nestlé: Nestlé's integrated report not only presents financial data but also underscores the company's commitment to addressing global challenges, such as malnutrition and environmental sustainability. It highlights the company's efforts to align its business strategy with societal needs, thus creating value for both the organization and its stakeholders. www.nestle.com/sustainability

Unilever: Unilever's report does a good job of demonstrating the connection between sustainability initiatives and financial performance. By detailing progress on reducing environmental impact, promoting diversity and inclusion, and enhancing the livelihoods of communities, Unilever shows how responsible business practices contribute to its long-term success. www.unilever.ca/

Coca-Cola: Coca-Cola's integrated report, an excellent example of an integrated report, showcases how the company is managing its water resources, advancing packaging sustainability, and engaging with local communities. By transparently sharing the environmental and social dimensions of its operations, Coca-Cola illustrates its commitment to mitigating risks and driving innovation. www. coca-colahellenic.com/en/investor-relations/2023-integrated-annual-report. The latest report can be found by googling 'coca cola integrated report.

Novartis: Novartis, the pharmaceutical company, was the winner of the Reuters Reporting and Transparency Award for their 2022 integrated report, which can be found at www.reporting.novartis .com/2022/novartis-in-society.html. Also the latest integrated report can be found by googling Novartis integrated report.

The judges for the Reuters Award said they consistently were producing high-quality, transparent reports, and they found that the company's innovation was impressive—especially their attempt to put a financial value (i.e., useful metrics) on the E initiatives in their ESG reporting. Novartis' work sets "an encouraging standard for future reporting practices for all businesses, markets and policy makers that we can in fact integrate sustainable measures into financial assessments."

The report included metrics/KPIs for:

- Energy use—on site and purchased
- Greenhouse gas (GHG) emissions
- Total Scope 1 emissions
- Combustion and process
- Total Scope 2 emissions (market-based)
- Total Scope 2 emissions (location-based)
- Total Scope 1 and Scope 2 (excluding offsets)
- Total Scope 3 emissions
- Purchased goods and services
- Capital goods
- Business travel
- Use of sold products
- Total Scope 1, Scope 2, and Scope 3 emissions
- Carbon offsets
- GHG emissions intensity (tCO_2e)
- Scope 1 and Scope 2 per million USD sales
- Scope 1 and Scope 2 per FTE

Integrating With Technology

Thanks to website technology like hyperlinks, data tagging, and so on, companies can readily link their core integrated reports with supplementary reports and data sets that users can custom-select and download as they choose. Indeed, the whole of chapter 7 of the book "One Report: Integrated Reporting for a Sustainable Strategy' by Eccles and Krzus, published by Wiley in October 2015 is devoted to the Internet and integrated reporting.

The Integrated Reporting Framework itself makes reference to linking in corporate websites in paragraph 1.16.

> An integrated report can provide an "entry point" to more detailed information outside the designated communication, to which it may be linked. The form of link will depend on the form of the integrated report (e.g., for a paper-based report, links may involve attaching other information as an appendix; for a web-based report, it may involve hyperlinking to that other information).

There is very little presentation of interactive data, that is, data in XBRL or other markup languages in corporate websites. Although XBRL is required for filings with the U.S. Securities and Exchange Commission, the information is presented in the same format as the old paper reports. The emphasis is on reading the individual reports, not on analyzing the data or information they actually contain.

Nevertheless, integrated reporting gives us a framework for assessing the direction that web-based reporting is likely to take. Since web-based reporting has become the primary vehicle of corporate reporting, then this really sheds a lot of light on the future of corporate reporting itself. Web-based reporting both simplifies the preparation of integrated reports and, at the same time, makes those reports more useful.

Although integrated reporting has been gaining some traction, it has not been widely adopted so far. At present, companies typically present financial reports and sustainability reports separately. In addition, the governance reports and, sometimes, the social reports are often presented separately from the environmental reports and often in different parts of the annual report or the website. In short, there is a lot of work to be done in the quest for widespread adoption of integrated reporting. And the underlying technology is continually changing.

In *The Future of Corporate Reporting—Creating the Dynamics for Change*,[2] a study published by The Federation of European Accountants, the following point is made:

> The corporate reporting of the future should take full account of changes in technology. Developments in the model for future corporate reporting should be flexible and able to adapt to changes in technology which affect the way people interact with an entity and which significantly affect the delivery of the information itself.[3]

The Integrated Reporting Framework as promulgated by the IIRC provides guidance on content but leaves a good bit of flexibility in how the integrated report is actually compiled.

Issues Raised by Integrated Reporting

Given the innovative nature of integrated reporting and the principles that have been adopted so far, there are several issues that need to be addressed and will be addressed as experience grows and standards develop further. The major issues are as follows:

- *Data Collection and Validation:* Gathering reliable nonfinancial data can be extremely complex and difficult due to the variety of sources of information and the lack of uniformity in the format of the data in these various sources. Organizations need robust data collection and validation processes to ensure the accuracy of information. This is especially important when assurance is required on the reports. Systems for gathering and processing reported information are an important part of the assurance process, and some jurisdictions require separate assurance reports on those systems.

- *Subjectivity:* Determining what integrated, as against combined, actually means. An "integrated report" provides information in a way that shows the relationships between the various elements of the report. But, the issue is, where do we cross the line between combined and integrated? How much relationship needs to be disclosed to make it an integrated report? These are subjective questions.
- *Materiality:* Another area of subjectivity is determining materiality, which involves assessing what aspects of an organization's ESG performance are significant enough to affect the decisions of stakeholders. BP (otherwise known as British Petroleum) approached this issue in 2004 by developing a materiality matrix, which was used to select and prioritize issues to be included in its sustainability report. Ford and BT followed a similar course by showing materiality matrixes in their sustainability reports.

This idea originated from the GRI standards, which recommend a matrix in which the X-axis is "Significance of Economic, Environmental, and Social Impacts" and the Y-axis is "Influence on Stakeholder Assessments and Decisions." Some firms choose to define the X-axis as "importance to the company" or something similar.

Mountain Equipment Co-op has a clear explanation of its materiality analysis: "At MEC, we use materiality analysis in two ways: to inform sustainability strategy by highlighting issues that matter to stakeholders and the organization and to inform reporting to ensure transparent communication about material issues."

- *Conciseness:* Integrating numerous data points into a single report may overwhelm readers, making it crucial to present information in a digestible format. This concern for conciseness has raised the issue in some minds that it will reduce the amount of information provided to stakeholders. However, there is already information overload in corporate reporting (look at the size of financial reports and sustainability reports), and concise integrated reports may be a way to enable stakeholders to focus on what's important.

- *Need for Stronger Standards:* Despite the IIRC framework, there's still a lack of consistent reporting standards across industries and regions. This can hinder comparability between organizations and allow space for greenwashing as well.

On the con side, integrated reports can take extra time to prepare, and time is already short in preparing traditional reports, particularly those required for regulatory purposes. A great deal of extra planning is required to prepare the reports, with greater collaboration between various departments of the company.

If the primary reports are not integrated themselves, but rather a separate integrated report is prepared, then the additional time can be wasted since there may be a tendency for people to concentrate on the traditional reports. Moreover, in cases where this approach is taken, there is a tendency for the integrated report to be presented in a summary form, which, as mentioned, can degrade the importance of the ESG factors.

In conclusion, integrated reporting is a dynamic approach that transcends the boundaries of traditional financial reporting. By providing a holistic view of an organization's operations, strategy, and value creation, integrated reports offer stakeholders a more comprehensive understanding of an organization's true performance in relation to the six capitals. While challenges such as data reliability and standardization persist, the ongoing evolution of integrated reporting practices holds the promise of enhancing transparency, accountability, and sustainable decision making in the corporate world.

Integrated Thinking

A wide consensus has emerged that for an organization to take into account all six capitals on an integrated basis, its thinking must become more integrated. In other words, decisions need to be made while including the impacts on financial, social, natural, and other capitals together. Such thinking must be included in the strategic and operational thinking of the organization to be effective. An example would be embedding the thinking into procurement decisions; what are the principles that drive procurement decisions—cost, carbon footprint, governance, or something else?

Integrated thinking is introduced in the Integrated Reporting Framework and further explained in the "Integrated Thinking Principles" issued by the Value Reporting Foundation, now consolidated into the IFRS Foundation. Full integrated thinking in the sense of being incorporated in all the corporate operational and strategic thinking is, as a practical matter, a long-term goal. However, a measure of integrated thinking is necessary in order to properly develop an integrated report. A new mindset is needed.

The Integrated Thinking document sets out six principles of integrated thinking and describes integrated thinking in terms of three layers of implementation. The six principles are as follows:

1. Purpose—the existence and contribution of the company to the needs of society and the environment.
2. Governance—the role of governance in value creation.
3. Culture—how corporate culture earns the trust of stakeholders and aligns with core values.
4. Strategy—how organizational objectives are to be met.
5. Risks and Opportunities—the impact of risks and opportunities on the business model.
6. Performance—how to measure and communicate value creation, which takes us into the idea of integrated reporting.

The principles of integrated thinking are necessarily related to the six capitals, which form the basis of integrated thinking, as shown in Figure 5.1. The principles are implemented for each of the six capitals at three levels:

1. "*The first level* of implementation (the principles) challenges those charged with governance to question how widely each of the six principles has been adopted across their organization.
2. *The second level (Assessment)* provides the executive management with a gauge to measure how deeply these principles have been embedded into day-to-day operations.
3. *The third level* (Operationalizing the principles) consists of a series of questions to be addressed by senior and middle management regarding management tools, practices and processes to bring integrated thinking to life."[4]

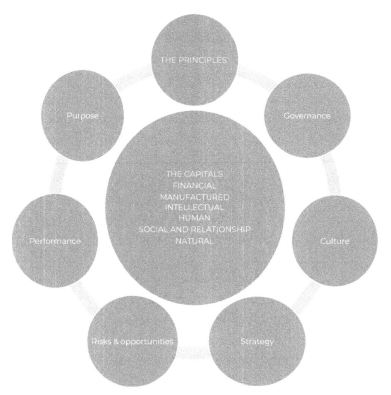

Figure 5.1 Integrated thinking relationships

Several case studies have been published by the Value Reporting Group,[‡] which shed light on how the principles and levels of implementation translate into the real world. Several points are made clear in the case studies. For example, sustainability cannot be separated from the corporate business model, and sustainability must be considered for all stages of the product life cycle.

BMW provided a good analysis of how they approached the implementation of integrated thinking. They developed their business model to incorporate all aspects of sustainability. Then they formed a single multifunctional team from across the organization to work together on a unified basis. They consulted with stakeholders and spoke with community

‡ www.integratedreporting.org/case-studies-from-the-business-networks-integrated-thinking-strategy-group/.

members, such as universities. They committed to including their supply chain in their thinking and actions.

Other large progressive companies, mostly European-based, such as Phillips and Novo Nordisk, have explored how to embed those sustainability elements into their business models, strategic thinking, and planning that they believed were central drivers of, or contributors to, business success, competitive advantage, resilience, stakeholder trust, and long-term value creation.

Such thinking, accompanied by new metrics and balanced scorecards, was conducive to improved management decision making and also called for deeper, more formal, systematic stakeholder engagement to identify issues important to a company's success. These companies saw this as an important step forward from just carrying out regulatory compliance and corporate social responsibility programs.

Integrated thinking goes a lot further than simply disclosures. There is much talk in the sustainability literature about integrated reporting needing integrated thinking, which integrates sustainability into the ongoing strategy and management of an organization. This is a comprehensive idea and if fully thought through and implemented can change the company.

Just as integrated reporting extends beyond financial reporting, integrated thinking extends beyond providing a basis for integrated reporting to the actual conduct of operational and strategic management. That leads us toward the field of Strategic Corporate Social Responsibility (CSR).

CHAPTER 6

Integrated Thinking and Beyond

The Opportunity

The adoption of integrated thinking presents a real opportunity for a company to plan its future. With integrated thinking, a company has drawn together its various skills and started them working together. The resultant team develops an outlook and new skills that can then be used for good purposes. The integrated thinking principles make it clear that integrated thinking is a journey, not a destination. That is no doubt true, especially with our rapidly changing world. Nevertheless, a company can use integrated thinking for its intended purpose for a time and decide it wants to move into new territory. Having the new integrated team and the new outlook it inevitably carries with it is where the opportunity for change lies.

But where does a company go from there? Do they just stay at the level where they are, or do they continue the integrated thinking journey, continuing to integrate the various parts of the organization and tweak the system in response to the changes that will inevitably become necessary? Perhaps, they would continue to improve their integrated reports. Or perhaps, they would move beyond a focus on corporate reporting to a greater focus on corporate strategy, where the emphasis on nonfinancial concerns takes on a more active tone, where actions are taken to actually do something about the nonfinancial ills in the world. Perhaps, they would adopt a new sense of social responsibility. Integrated thinking provides a solid base for adopting a strategy of corporate social responsibility (CSR).

Shifting the Thinking

As we have seen, integrated thinking involves a fundamental change in corporate thinking. Moving beyond integrated thinking to strategic

CSR requires another fundamental shift in thinking, from a focus on broadening the reporting process of the company to broadening the entire strategy and operations of the company. The change means a focus on factors that benefit society as a whole; indeed, the world as a whole, rather than, or in addition to, optimizing value creation for the six capitals. As with integrated thinking, CSR should not lead to lower returns for shareholders on their investment, but rather in the longer term, companies are more likely to achieve higher returns and have greater success in attracting and retaining top talent. If sustainability factors are addressed along the way, then the negative effects of not addressing them when serious events take place are less likely to be experienced.

Integrated thinking means bringing together the various parts, departments, areas, and people in an organization to focus on common goals other than what they might have focused on in the past. For example, the finance function in an organization is normally focused on money: generating it and managing it. Profits are central. They need to respond to the scrutiny of the media and analysts, who set expectations as to the profit levels and growth of the organization. When these expectations are not met, their share prices on the stock market suffer in value. When they are met or exceeded, the impact on share prices is preserved. All of this has an important impact on the ability of the company to raise capital at reasonable prices. So naturally, the finance function as well as top management pay close attention to the predictions and responses of the analysts and the press. This has been a fundamental aspect of corporate management for many decades. The impact it has on management is profound. It forces management into short-term thinking since the interaction of market forces takes place very quickly. And since the reactions of analysts and the press are very public, they are a matter of considerable concern to top management.

As previously discussed, the concerns of the public, many investors, and analysts have shifted to include matters relating to the environment, social impact, and governance. Much attention has been given to climate-related issues in particular, whether it be atmospheric, water pollution, or impact on the landscape. Also, questions around equality, diversity, and fairness in governance have dominated the news for several years, and companies that do a good job of, say, diversity will gain recognition and perhaps a premium on the market. The approach to profits is still much the same since profits are necessary to yield good returns on investments, while companies also meet sustainability expectations.

The trend to integrated thinking has enabled many companies to respond to these demands by setting strategies that incentivize the various key parts of the organization to work together on common sustainable goals as well as their own traditional areas. With integrated thinking, however, the focus is on the effect of events on the six capitals in play in the organization. There is, therefore, a limitation on the scope of the interaction since sustainability goals can have a considerable effect on other aspects of the company.

Moving to a full strategic CSR focus can serve to broaden the scope of the social elements of decision making, always remembering that profits must be earned and that the full serving of social concerns can only be fully met if there is a good profitability record. Simply, it is back to making enough money to allow the company to invest in other areas such as environmental restoration, replanting, social investments in people (education, fair pay, apprenticeships for young people), and adhering to the highest ethical standards in how they do business.

There is always this balancing act. But there is a good deal of judgment in this approach. How far do we go? How do we know when we are getting off track? Adoption of CSR in itself may not help in addressing this issue but does require that it be addressed. Corporate objectives are key and they must be measurable and the companies need to have a frame of reference to guide the setting of those objectives.

Some Possible Directions

One of the approaches taken by some companies is that of using the United Nations sustainability development goals (SDGs) as a benchmark in setting objectives and priorities. Included in "The 2030 Agenda for Sustainable Development," adopted by all United Nations Member States in 2015, the goals provide a shared blueprint for peace and prosperity for people and the planet, now and into the future." It's obvious in reading

---

* https://sdgs.un.org/goals.

them that no one company, person, or country could possibly achieve these goals themselves, but they can help. Companies such as BMW (discussed later) have used these goals in setting their objectives for their integrated thinking program, and others are using them for their CSR program. These goals, generally referred to as the 17 UN SDGs, are:

1. *No Poverty*—End poverty in all its forms everywhere

   According to Chandler, "If current long-term trend lines of economic growth continue, we will see abject poverty almost completely eradicated in the 21st century. Business is not a zero-sum game struggling over a fixed pie. Instead, it grows and makes the total pie larger, creating value for all of its major stakeholders—customers, employees, suppliers, investors and communities.[1]"

   Considerable poverty comes from inequality, where some people who are better off do well, and others who are barely getting by are often going without food and shelter. While there will always be some inequality, a major problem arises when inequality becomes too large, leading to social unrest, riots, and political turmoil.

2. *Zero Hunger*—End hunger, achieve food security and improved nutrition, and promote sustainable agriculture.

   Worldwide, the issue of food scarcity is well documented. Opportunities for companies come at the local level, where even just running a good profitable business will be good for the community economically. The opportunities also come when the company operates in different countries, some of which may have greater economic problems than others. In those cases, the company can support or launch various programs to help with the situation.

   The choice of CSR objectives depends not so much on how the company spends money but on how it makes money. The area of zero hunger is a good example of this principle. If a company is in the business of food production and retailing, such as Loblaws or Kraft or Nestle, then by virtue of their product, they would naturally help with addressing hunger. If they make their product available in needy areas at reasonable prices that people can afford or through

National Food Programs groups, then they will be doing even more about addressing hunger. Perhaps they could invest in teaching agricultural techniques to local communities to increase yield in the emerging economies where they do business.

3. *Good Health and Well-being*—Ensure healthy lives and promote well-being for everyone at all ages.

This is also an area that shows the wisdom of choosing how the company makes money, but it also offers some good examples of how to spend money for good CSR purposes. Suppose a company offers a chain of fitness salons where people can go and exercise and perhaps also obtain healthful natural food products. They can also lend their logo and some resources to support local sports teams, which involves spending money to promote good health and well-being. This, of course, is common and provides good PR for the company.

4. *Quality Education*—Ensure inclusive and equitable quality education and promote lifelong learning opportunities for all. Companies offer support for good education in different ways, such as providing scholarship programs, sending their experts to speak at universities and schools, and supporting employees who wish to gain a better education.

5. *Gender Equality*—Achieve gender equality and empower all women and girls.

Many companies are working hard to address this area, including adoption of neutral hiring practices, working toward gender equality on the board and in management positions, and adoption of practices to support pregnancy leaves.

6. *Clean Water and Sanitation*—Ensure availability and sustainable management of water and sanitation for all. Many companies use water or discharge waste into bodies of water. How they do that can define the quality of their CSR practices. Do they take steps to preserve the pure water they use in a sustainable way, and do they ensure that their effluent is not a hazard to the community?

7. *Affordable and Clean Energy*—Ensure access to affordable, reliable, sustainable, and modern energy for all. Some companies are in the business of providing clean and affordable energy by selling

wood and wood chips, propane and electric vehicles (such as Tesla). In these cases, their prime line of business serves to promote this cause, provided it is done with care and attention to good sustainable practices.

8. *Decent Work and Economic Growth*—Promote sustained, inclusive, and sustainable economic growth, full and productive employment, and decent work for all. This is a good example of combining growth goals and sustainability goals. It recognizes that economic growth is not inconsistent with providing good working conditions. Indeed, the relationship is such that growth is supported by good working conditions.

9. *Industry, Innovation, and Infrastructure*—Build resilient infrastructure, promote inclusive and sustainable industrialization, and foster innovation. Most companies recognize that building strong infrastructure is good business and do so when economic and business opportunities warrant.

10. *Reduced Inequalities*—Reduce inequality within and among countries. Multinational companies have a unique opportunity to work toward greater equality in the countries in which they operate. This can be approached through hiring and employment practices, basically trying to improve the lot of the local people they employ and otherwise work with.

11. *Sustainable Cities and Communities*—Make cities and human settlements inclusive, safe, resilient, and sustainable. Inclusivity is a hallmark of the modern company. Working with the communities can be a productive and helpful way to assist in the development of those communities to be safe, inclusive, resilient, and sustainable. This area covers a lot of ground.

12. *Responsible Consumption and Production*—Ensure sustainable consumption and production patterns. Sustainability can be built into products, such as through sustainable packaging and delivery.

13. *Climate Action*—Take urgent action to combat climate change and its impacts. Most companies accomplish this through controlled emissions and waste.

14. *Life Below Water*—Conserve and sustainably use the oceans, seas, and marine resources for sustainable development. Waterways, in

particular the oceans, have suffered tremendously in recent years, with such pollution as plastic floating in waters around the world. Recent sailing racers in the North Atlantic commented in 2023 that they were surprised at how much plastic they saw floating on the water. And we know that particles of plastic are injuring and killing numerous fish species. Companies can help by controlling or limiting their plastic waste products.

15. *Life on Land*—Protect, restore, and promote sustainable use of terrestrial ecosystems, sustainably manage forests, combat desertification, and halt and reverse land degradation and halt biodiversity loss. Many companies work with land and forests and can take steps to protect them.

16. *Peace, Justice, and Strong Institutions*—Promote peaceful and inclusive societies for sustainable development, provide access to justice for all, and build effective, accountable, and inclusive institutions at all levels. Many companies support societies that work to promote sustainable development.

17. *Partnerships*—Strengthen the means of implementation and revitalize the global partnership for sustainable development. Partnerships, particularly multistakeholder alliances, will make a contribution to this laudable goal. No one company can accomplish all these goals by itself, but working with others is a sensible approach. On the other hand, most companies need to optimize their use of time, which would influence any action in this regard.

The UN sustainability goals are a very broad set of guidelines which no profit-oriented company could fully adopt. Nor would they have the time to address them all. They are guiding principles or ideas for how stakeholders should/could conduct their business (from companies to investors and everything in between). Most companies can consider them in formulating their corporate strategies and, in combination with their profit and growth goals, look for opportunities to adopt those goals that would be most compatible with their financial strategies. They do provide a useful source to guide the company's direction.

For example, the BMW Group has a long tradition of publishing environmental reports, disclosing the impact of its operations on the environment, including mitigating measures. In 2015, when the General Assembly of the UN announced their 17 SDGs,

> the (BMW) Group identified the SDGs to which it can make a direct and thus the greatest possible contribution with its own sustainability goals. After the Board of Management redefined the company's central sustainability goals in 2020, including reducing the lifecycle CO_2 emissions per vehicle by at least a third by 2030 and measuring the progress of BMW's journey towards carbon neutrality by 2050 using science-based targets.[†]

The SDGs can be used, such as in the case of BMW, for integrated thinking but are also perhaps even more appropriate for strategic CSR. As previously discussed, both integrated thinking and CSR can vary widely, sometimes being very similar and in other cases being quite different. The use of the SDGs would normally draw the two closer together. However, integrated thinking and CSR have somewhat different orientations.

The Value Reporting Foundation, the originator of integrated thinking, is focused on enterprise value in all its forms—how it is created, preserved, or eroded over time. It is devoted to moving away from the traditional view of enterprise value as a financial concept to the value represented by the six capitals built into integrated reporting.

At the same time, CSR has moved from the concept of "giving back to society" toward a concept of *how* value is created by a firm, and what the environmental, social, and governmental (including ethical) implications of the value-creating processes are—how the money is made. A good example of how value is created can be found in how employees are treated: whether they are paid fair wages and provided good working conditions. If not, then it can be concluded that the company is creating value on the backs of, and at the expense of, its employees. "If a company relies on low-priced finished products to gain an edge over its competitors, it implicitly depends on the exploitation of workers who are paid below minimum wages."[2]

[†] Integrated Thinking in Action, A Spotlight on the BMG Group, Case Study, Value Reporting Foundation.

Both integrated thinking and CSR are intended to be established at a strategic level and integrated into the business strategy and related processes, including throughout its supply chains. "As Kim and Davis (2016: p.1897) have pointed out, 'Nike shoes, Apple phones, and Hewlett-Packard laptops are all manufactured by far-flung contractors, not by the company whose logo is engraved on the product.'"[3]

The major difference between integrated thinking and strategic CSR is that integrated thinking is directed toward measuring and reporting on value creation, whereas CSR is directed toward structuring the organization so as to maximize or optimize value creation and serving social needs. Moreover, decisions made in determining appropriate strategies for integrated thinking are likely to be made in the context of what should/can be reported to stakeholders. In contrast, CSR is rooted in the idea that the company should be serving the needs of the society as best as it can, an idea of social consciousness. Therefore, CSR is likely to have a more sweeping impact on corporate strategy.

The question of what lies beyond integrated thinking leads naturally to strategic CSR since both are rooted in strategy, with one being broader than the other. This is the subject of the next chapter.

CHAPTER 7

Strategic Corporate Social Responsibility

Definition of CSR

Noteworthy within the extensive literature in both academic and business publications on corporate social responsibility (CSR) are the writings of Peter Drucker in 1974 and later, and Archie B Carroll in 1992. They placed an emphasis on what has been called strategic CSR, which means that CSR is incorporated into the corporate culture and strategy.

Yet, there is some confusion around whether there are differences between integrated thinking and CSR, and if there are, what those differences might be. Some say that integrated thinking is the same as CSR or a form of it. There is some truth in the latter, since CSR exists in a wide range of activities, from using petty cash for buying Guide Cookies to corporate philanthropy to developing broad-ranging strategies that address all the various areas of interest or capital. The broad range of CSR can easily embrace integrated thinking.

In the past, CSR has often been practised on an ad hoc basis, responding to particular events and pressures. The trouble with this kind of CSR is that it simply is driven by responding to pressures from stakeholders and therefore tends to result in short-term activities that may not necessarily fit with the other business strategies of the company. Also, the CSR activities essentially become a form of PR and may do little good for society or ESG needs.

Strategic CSR, on the other hand, is driven by strategic planning and, more importantly, fits into the strategic business goals of the company. It may be the general corporate strategic planning or a strategic planning exercise specific to CSR. Either way, the result is that the CSR activities are more likely to be proactive and to fit with the overall strategic imperatives of the company. They are also more likely to be long-term strategies and have more lasting results. Strategic CSR is the closest version of CSR to integrated thinking.

According to David Chandler, "In defining strategic CSR, five components are essential:

(1) that firms incorporate a CSR perspective in their culture and strategic planning process,
(2) that any actions taken are directly related to core operations,
(3) that firms seek to understand and respond to the needs of their stakeholders,
(4) that they aim to optimize value created, and
(5) that they shift from a short-term perspective to managing relations with key stakeholders over the medium to long term.[1]"

In 2001, the European Commission proposed its first definition of CSR. In a green paper, it is stated that CSR is "a concept whereby companies integrate social and environmental concerns in their business operations and in their interaction with their stakeholders on a voluntary basis."[2]

Despite all the literature on the definition of CSR, there has not been total agreement on exactly what it is. Perhaps the most meaningful definition of CSR is found in the Guide to Corporate Sustainability published by the United Nations Global Compact (UNGC). Their definition of corporate sustainability is really that of CSR. It is defined according to five actions that companies must take to meet the standard of sustainability and become a member of the global compact. The five actions:

1. Operate with integrity, respecting fundamental responsibilities in the areas of human rights, labor, environment, and anticorruption.
2. Look beyond their own walls and take actions to support the societies around them on issues such as poverty, conflict, an uneducated workforce, and resource scarcity.
3. Make a public commitment by the chief executive, with support from the board of directors.

4. Produce an annual progress communication, typically as part of their sustainability or annual report that provides "the company's stakeholders with an account of their efforts to operate responsibly and support society."
5. Participate in local communities.

These five actions feed into the 10 principles[*] of the UNGC, which are:

Human Rights

1. Businesses should support and respect the protection of internationally proclaimed human rights;
2. and make sure that they are not complicit in human rights abuses.

Labor

3. Businesses should uphold the freedom of association and the effective recognition of the right to collective bargaining;
4. the elimination of all forms of forced and compulsory labor;
5. the effective abolition of child labor; and
6. the elimination of discrimination in respect of employment and occupation.

Environment

7. Businesses should support a precautionary approach to environmental challenges;
8. undertake initiatives to promote greater environmental responsibility; and

---

[*] The 10 principles of the United Nations Global Compact are derived from: the Universal Declaration of Human Rights, the International Labour Organization's Declaration on Fundamental Principles and Rights at Work, the Rio Declaration on Environment and Development, and the United Nations Convention Against Corruption.

9. encourage the development and diffusion of environmentally friendly technologies.

Anticorruption

10. Businesses should work against corruption in all its forms, including extortion and bribery.

More than 18,000 companies and 3,800 nonbusiness signatories based in over 160 countries and 62 local networks have adopted the principles, making the UNGC the world's largest corporate sustainability initiative. The UNGC states that the principles-based approach means taking responsibility for the company's actions in the areas of human rights, labor, environment, and anticorruption. They state that incorporating the 10 principles into their strategies, policies, and procedures "and establishing a culture of integrity, companies are not only upholding their basic responsibilities to people and the planet, but also setting the stage for long-term success."

Transitioning From Integrated Thinking

A company that has developed an integrated thinking strategy in order to adopt integrated reporting has a good start for developing a strategic CSR strategy. Strategic CSR also provides a good umbrella under which to refine and operate an integrated thinking strategy because CSR is much broader than integrated thinking, which is specifically directed to the six capitals of integrated reporting and is generally adopted primarily to provide support for integrated reporting. But there are benefits to adopting a CSR perspective because it is based on the recognition of a responsibility for corporate behavior as opposed to the more limited goal of providing effective integrated reports. With the adoption of a CSR perspective, integrated thinking can still be developed but is more likely to encompass the broad strategic and operational perspective that is needed for an effective result in the broader range of corporate activities. Also, it is good to adopt a CSR perspective to take full advantage of the extensive thinking and research that has gone into CSR over the years.

CSR Versus Profits

Clearly, the objectives of CSR are not to eliminate or reduce the for-profit activities of corporations. The profit motive is at the core of modern democratic societies, and the resources thus generated are extremely beneficial to society. It can be seen from history that the profit motive has changed and oscillated over the centuries, but it never disappeared. Even when the companies were set up to meet the objectives of the governments, such as the Roman Republic wanting them to create and manage their armies to the British Crown wanting them to establish relations with their colonies, the ability to earn profits was always a necessary factor in achieving success in those endeavors.

Similarly, the earning of profits in companies adopting CSR is essential to being able to achieve the objectives of CSR itself. Companies cannot adopt policies to reduce their impact on the environment if they do not have the money to finance the necessary activities. They cannot do the best job of providing payment to their employees if they do not earn the profits to be able to finance that remuneration.

Business managers often state that CSR is an ideal but that the purpose of the business is to make a profit, thus implying or stating that there is an inconsistency between the two. The economic argument in particular, but also the others, serves to argue against this position and points out that profit making is not only not inconsistent with CSR but adds to and supports it. Some, such as Larry Fink of Blackrock, say that a CSR mindset is actually more profitable (than a non-CSR mindset).[†]

When a company makes decisions prompted by the profit motive, they are not necessarily contrary to good social values or detrimental to society. Quite the contrary. A company might make a decision, for example, to cut out a segment of its business, perhaps a whole department, because the segment is performing poorly or losing money. That might lead to a decision to reassign staff or let some of them go. Of course, this might make life hard for the staff involved, but it also strengthens the company, making it possible to grow and prosper and ultimately hire

---

[†] www.morningstar.com/articles/1075068/larry-fink-sustainable-investing-is-about-profits-not-taking-a-stand.

more people. A bankrupt company is of no value to anyone. A company that is CSR aware would recognize the difficulties of the people who were let go, and do what it can to help them through their transition, perhaps through good severance pay, provision of training for new positions, and effective counseling programs that offer real help in finding new work and coping with the transition.

On the other side of employee relations, the company may decide that it must raise the wages of certain personnel. Most often, aside from regular periodic increments, this will happen only if major stakeholders of the company take a strong position that wage levels are too low and need to be adjusted or if there is legislative or regulatory intervention or strong strike action.

> It is essential to realize that the firm is not raising its wages out of some well—intentioned social altruism, but due to a shift in business fundamentals. And the stakeholder endorsement is an essential component of that: it allows the firm to know that the change is a good business decision, rather than one that potentially damages its economic viability. The point is that, ultimately, firms do not define our societal values; they reflect them. For-profit firms are very good at providing us with what we actually want (rather than what we say we want).[3]

Who Are the Stakeholders

As mentioned earlier, the stakeholders of a company are varied and diverse. They include the shareholders, who own a part of the equity in the company and, therefore, are very tied to the success or otherwise of the company overall. They include the creditors, such as banks, who are dependent on the success of the company to achieve repayment. And they include the employees, customers, and suppliers, all of whom depend on the company for their livelihood, or at least part of it.

Corporate stakeholders include employees, customers, communities, governments, creditors, debtors, trade associations, and others. Communities, in particular, include the immediate communities in which the facilities of a company are located. But communities also include the broader communities such as the states (or provinces) and countries in which the companies operate. Governments are stakeholders because they need the tax revenue from the companies in their jurisdiction, also they need to monitor that they are following the laws of the land and are not adopting activities that will endanger or seriously offend the people and thus raise political issues that they would need to deal with. Trade associations want to know that their members are following proper rules of trade with good ethical practices. Not only is their membership level at stake but also their reputation and standing in the community.

All of these groups have shown a growing interest in the ESG record of companies. The interests of the stakeholders vary considerably, and overall, their interests clearly extend well beyond the profitability of the company to the manner in which they do business and the nature of their involvement in their communities. A strong CSR strategy is an effective way to deal with these concerns.

Why Adopt CSR?

We have already discussed some of the broader reasons for adopting CSR in terms of satisfying stakeholders. However, the arguments for adopting CSR fall into various categories, including ethical, moral, rational, and economic.

Ethical

This stream of thought is closely aligned with utilitarianism, which was most famously advocated by the 18th-century English political philosopher Jeremy Bentham, who argued that "an action is considered ethical … when the action is intended to produce the greatest net benefit (or lowest net cost) to society when compared to all the other alternatives."[4]

In Bentham's definition, producing the greatest new benefit to society is more than the economic benefit but would include all the other factors relating to sustainability. If there are several ways to achieve corporate objectives in profits, but they vary in their impact on society, then choosing the one that has the best overall effect on society would be the most ethical path to follow. It would also be the path most likely to satisfy all the stakeholders. A CSR strategy is a good way to achieve this ethical standard.

Moral

The moral argument goes something like this. Businesses and society interact together all the time. Society contributes to the economic and social environment in which the business operates. Since society continually contributes to business, business has a responsibility to do likewise. The economic and social environment is crucial to the successful operations of a company. This would include reasonable rates of taxation, stable government, low crime rates, and decent living conditions for their people. Many businesses have left a location because the social or economic environment has deteriorated to the point that it is not adequate to support the business. And many businesses have located or relocated their facilities to places having a better economic and social environment than their current location.

Rational

The rational argument for adopting CSR: "A loss of societal legitimacy can lead to a rise in the countervailing forces of strikes (employees), activism (NGOs), boycotts (consumers), legislation (government), or bad press (media) that constrain the firm's ability to act."[5]

This is the "actions have consequences" rule. If a company acts in a way that ignores or downplays the legitimate concerns or interests in society, then some part of that society, whether it be associations, people, or mobs will eventually react. Such reactions can be unpredictable and detrimental to the company in various degrees. Inaction has consequences, too.

Economic

The economic argument for the adoption of CSR rests on the idea that a business must satisfy the needs of its stakeholders in order to succeed. This creates more value for the stakeholders. It also offers an opportunity to differentiate itself from competitors. Even if the competitors adopt CSR, there is an opportunity to do it a different way. It also facilitates the building of positive relationships, which of course is good for business. The best way for a firm to make a profit over the medium to long term is to meet the needs of its stakeholders.

> CSR is central to business success because it provides firms with a set of operating principles around which their multiple stakeholders can rally. Equally, those stakeholders, in aggregate, form the context in which firms operate, rewarding actions of which they approve and punishing actions of which they disapprove.[6]

Strategies to satisfy the stakeholders should be proactive rather than reactive.

These different arguments are more than philosophical ramblings. In fact, the particular argument that a business adopts will determine the nature of the CSR policies it follows. For example, the argument that the adoption of CSR can create economic opportunities is clearly illustrated in the case of Toyota. The company responded earlier than others to concerns about fuel emissions by developing the Prius hybrid engine. That initiative gave Toyota a significant lead over its competitors in hybrid technology and at the same time enabled a significant reduction in pollutants for the benefit of society.

Legal

Laws around the world are quickly evolving, particularly with regard to sustainability.

There has recently been a resurgence of new governmental laws and regulations that specifically address CSR, such as the EU directive on nonfinancial reporting or U.S. regulations against corruption (Kourula et al. 2019).[7] The EU, the United States, and many other jurisdictions have passed laws on social and environmental reporting, handling of conflict materials, and offering or accepting bribes in another country (e.g., the U.S. Foreign Corrupt Practices Act). There are many other examples.

> International organizations play an important role. This includes the United Nations (particularly the UNGC), the OECD, the ILO and the World Bank, all of which have embarked on the CSR

agenda and have proposed ideas and policies that generally aim to establish global rules for private actors, so-called soft law.[8]

The Driving Forces of CSR

Chandler defines five driving forces of CSR—affluence, sustainability, globalization, communication, and brands[9]:

1. Affluence—Some degree of affluence is necessary for the effective implementation of CSR. Generally, the greater the level of affluence, the greater the ability to implement it, and also the greater the demand will be for it. Often, if the company is doing very well financially, the community will demand more in terms of social and other contributions because "they can afford it."

2. Sustainability—One of the major driving forces in the search for implementing CSR in businesses is clearly that of sustainability. Chandler provides a long view. "The first billion people accumulated over a leisurely interval, from the origins of humans hundreds of thousands of years ago to the early 1800s. Adding the second billion took another 120 or so years. Then, in the last 50 years, humanity more than doubled, surging from three billion in 1959 to four billion in 1974, five billion in 1987 and six billion in 1998.... The United Nations Population Division anticipates 8 billion people by 2025, 9 billion by 2043 and 10 billion by 2083.[10]"

   The plethora of climate incidents over recent years as already mentioned provides ample evidence of this strain on resources.

3. Globalization—The main feature of globalization from the viewpoint of an individual company is that they are operating in a wide variety of countries, with different laws, customs, social pressures, levels of stability, and economic needs. This forces the company to consider these differences. CSR is very helpful in this endeavor. It provides a very good framework in which to develop strategies that will make it possible to respond to the differences in a meaningful way and to help avoid embarrassing situations and legal violations.

4. Communication——Modern communication through digital means is incredibly fast, and such speed of communication facilitates com-

merce. The volume of e-mail and video downloads is sufficient to boggle the mind. "This technology enables communication among activist groups and like-minded individuals, empowering them to spread their message and providing the means to coordinate action."[11] Therefore, people and groups who oppose certain kinds of behavior or want companies to change their ways can communicate rapidly and form protest mobs quickly and efficiently.

5. Brands—Companies spend large amounts of money and effort to establish their brands. People will go to the brands they know, which makes them a crucial draw for business. However, due to shifting expectations, the complexity of business in a global environment and the ability of stakeholders to spread the news of "missteps" instantaneously to a global audience, a firm's reputation is increasingly precarious—hard to establish and easy to lose. "Brands therefore drive CSR because they raise the stakes—those that are trusted by stakeholders will be more successful in the market than those that are not."[12]

Effects of CSR on Behavior

The purpose of CSR is to guide the company in activities that result in achieving outcomes that are of greatest benefit to society and the company. Therefore, the CSR strategies are intended to influence the behavior of the company. This happens in various areas of the company and its management.

1. *Financial Benefits and Long-Term Sustainability*: Contrary to the misconception that CSR efforts hinder profitability, numerous studies have demonstrated a positive correlation between corporate social responsibility and financial performance. Sustainable practices, such as energy efficiency, waste reduction, and responsible sourcing, can lead to significant cost savings.

2. *Profit Maximization Shift*: Corporate strategies regarding profits may change from profit maximization to profit optimization.

3. *Marketing Strategy*: By actively engaging in socially responsible practices, businesses can build a positive brand image and gain public trust. Because stakeholders are increasingly concerned about the ethical and sustainable practices of the companies they support,

companies that prioritize CSR are more likely to attract loyal customers and enhance their market position. Marketing strategies can
be specifically directed to those stakeholders.

4. *Employee Engagement and Retention*: Adopting CSR initiatives can
significantly affect employee behavior within organizations. CSR
programs can provide employees with a sense of purpose, leading to
increased engagement, higher job satisfaction, and improved retention rates. Moreover, socially responsible companies tend to attract
talented individuals who are passionate about making a positive
impact on society and the environment.

5. *Positive Influence on Supply Chains*: CSR extends beyond internal
practices to the entire supply chain. Companies that embrace CSR
are inclined to ensure that their suppliers and partners adhere to ethical and sustainable practices as well. For example, Mountain Equipment Company (MEC), a Canadian sporting store company, has a
responsible sourcing policy.

The policy covers MEC label products as well other products
from other brands they sell. Responsible sourcing sets up MEC
to operate according to their values, and also makes sure they
manage risks, do not break any laws, and maintain good relationships with other businesses and suppliers. MEC ensures the
factories commit to MECs supplier code of conduct. Regular
audits are undertaken to ensure that the suppliers are upholding
the standards.[13]

CHAPTER 8

How to Implement Strategic Corporate Social Responsibility

We have seen that fundamental changes are required to implement integrated thinking and strategic CSR. They would require changes in the behavior of personnel in the business carrying out any functions relative to sustainability matters as well as finance personnel. It would be necessary for them to work together through a common understanding of the direction being taken by the company. The change process generally used in strategic planning with some tweaking would be an appropriate way to implement the required changes.

Strategic Planning for Sustainability

Business strategy formulation has long been a moving target as conditions change and society evolves. In recent years, more attention has been given to sustainability issues, both in terms of reporting and strategy.

SWOT

A common approach to strategy for years has been that of the SWOT analysis (Figure 8.1). It's still a popular model for strategy formulation, and most people are familiar with it. Basically, SWOT involves identifying the strengths, weaknesses, opportunities, and threats to a company in a particular scenario. These elements are then weighed to determine the best strategy to follow, utilizing the strengths, seizing the opportunities, mitigating the weaknesses, and avoiding the threats. SWOT is very open-ended and flexible and can be used in almost any situation, calling for

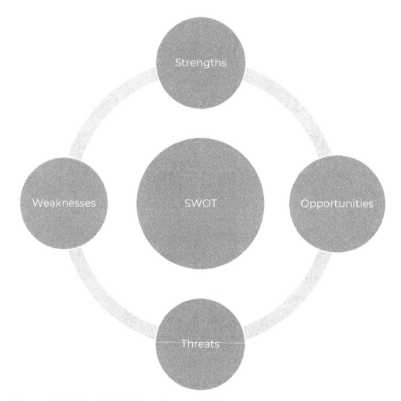

Figure 8.1 The SWOT analysis model

decisions to be made. As a result, it can be used in making decisions about sustainability and is used for that purpose.

A variation on SWOT is the sSWOT, or sustainability SWOT, a tool created by the World Resources Institute.[1] It is designed to use SWOT to address environmental challenges in cooperation with buyers, suppliers, and other stakeholders. The suggested approach is to identify the major environmental issues that are likely to be relevant to the company or its environment. The company might apply its known strengths to address those issues. Opportunities could include the alliances the company has and how they can be deployed to help with the issues. It's not hard to see how the various environmental issues could generate threats, strengths, weaknesses, and opportunities. And all of this can be considered in conjunction with the other regular SWOT items of the company on an integrated basis.

SWOT can be very useful. However, it is flexible and open-ended, which are both advantages and disadvantages.

Porter's Five Forces Model

It's the open-endedness and flexibility of SWOT, more particularly its lack of direction in charting a strategy, that led Michael Porter of Harvard University to develop his five forces model in 1979 (before sustainability became much of an issue) (Figure 8.2).

The Porter model is really an attempt to define the competitive environment of the company. In using it, the planner needs to identify the buyers' and suppliers' power, the risk of new entrants into competition with the company, the degree of rivalry among existing competitors, and the threat of substitutes in products and services. Like the SWOT model, the Porter model can be used in making sustainability decisions. Because

Figure 8.2 Porter's five forces model

of its clearer focus, it can provide a little more direction in sustainability decisions, although the sSWOT model does provide a little more direction than basic SWOT in making such decisions.

For example, the strength of buyers has been considerably enhanced in recent years, as they often wish to buy from companies that do business in accordance with their values. If they find, for example, the company is producing goods from the labor of children or people earning little or no pay, then they may refuse to buy the product. Also, suppliers may not wish to deal with the company for similar reasons arising, for example, from differences in approaches to employment issues.

Rivalry among existing competitors can also be affected for reasons similar to those of doing business with buyers and suppliers. The manner in which a company responds to sustainability issues may be sufficiently different in the eyes of customers that it would affect their decisions as to who they do business with.

Accordingly, the five forces model can provide a useful framework for considering the impact of sustainability issues in the strategic planning process.

Integrated Thinking

The concept of integrated thinking is also a way of modifying business strategy to accommodate sustainability issues. Integrated thinking, as shown in Figure 8.3, covers many of the same issues addressed in SWOT analysis and the five forces, such as risks (threats) and opportunities. But it also more specifically covers a wider range of sustainability issues, such as governance and social matters. Therefore, it provides more direction in the planning exercise than the other techniques of planning.

The six capitals sweep in a variety of sustainability issues and are used as a framework for the business model. The principles are applied to the business model. The risks and opportunities principle involves assessing the interaction of the business with the outside world, including the environment, geopolitical factors, and stakeholders. The strategy principle involves setting specific processes and strategies that serve the interests of the business model as well as addressing the areas where the business model intersects with the United Nations' SDGs within the overall

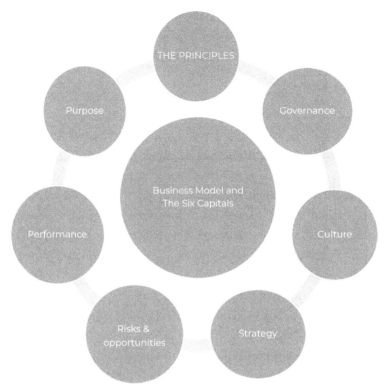

Figure 8.3 Integrated thinking

framework of the integrated thinking principles as defined by the Value
Reporting Foundation.

The various principles interact to enable the formulation of a cohesive
set of strategies and processes that will enable the achievement of the
organizational goals.

Corporate Social Responsibility

Strategic CSR starts with integrating social, environmental, and governance considerations into a company's overall business strategy, creating
a positive impact on both society and the organization itself. While it
may seem daunting, companies felt the same when SOX/52-109 programs were implemented for Internal Controls over Financial Reporting
(ICFR), but it was achieved, and while this is much broader and more
far-reaching, several of the basic operational activities to get there will be

similar, requiring top-down leadership involvement, careful coordination of different groups, setting of targets and controls, monitoring, and so on.

Strategic planning for CSR generally involves the following steps:

Define the Vision

A clear vision is necessary to begin the planning process and set the tone for the company's new CSR policy. This begins by identifying the purpose and values of the company, as well as its challenges and opportunities. By aligning the CSR strategy with the company's core business objectives, it becomes an integral part of the organizational culture and decision-making processes. From the vision, the objectives of the organization can be derived by linking the operations of the company to the overall elements of the vision.

A good starting point for developing a new vision is to adopt the 10 principles of the UN Global Compact (UNGC) and the UNGC Management Model (Figure 8.4). The principles cover human rights, labor, environment, and anticorruption. The management model is a guide to help companies incorporate the principles into their corporate strategies

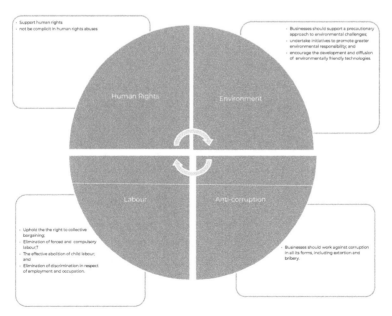

Figure 8.4 Corporate social responsibility—the UNGC management model

and operations. The more specific goals that need to be developed can be derived from the UN SDGs, which were outlined in the previous chapter.

The model was designed, as per the UNGC, to be practical, scalable, and straightforward. It sets out six management steps, which companies can use and continuously monitor to improve their alignment with the 10 principles. The steps which would be taken into consideration in the strategic planning process are as follows:

1. *Commit* to adopting the principles into strategy and operations.
2. *Assess* risks, opportunities, and impacts.
3. *Define* goals, strategies, and policies.
4. *Implement* strategies and policies.
5. *Measure* and monitor impacts and progress.
6. *Communicate* progress and strategies and engage with stakeholders.

Several companies start their CSR journey by defining their vision in terms of a social purpose or social value statement. Such a beginning forces the company to think about how it can approach its implementation of CSR. For example, Maple Leaf Mills, a very well-known Canadian company in the business of making and selling protein food products such as bacon and other packaged meats has identified its social purpose by using the slogan "Raise the Good in Food." Further, its social purpose statement reads, "We're a carbon neutral food company on a purposeful journey to 'Raise the Good in Food' through better nutrition, safer food and workplaces, more humane animal care, and sustainability efforts that protect our planet."*

As another example, Royal Dutch Shell emphasizes its role beyond the pursuit of its core business interests (the extraction and sale of fossil resources) to enhancing the security of supply and energy efficiency and promoting research, development, and introduction of alternative fuels.

Identify the Points of Intersection

To develop a suitable CSR strategy, it is necessary to narrow down the thinking from the overall issues facing society, such as those represented

---

* www.mapleleaffoods.com/.

by the UN goals. This is generally done by identifying the points of intersection between those broad societal goals and the activities of the company. There are two basic ways to approach this task—from the inside out and from the outside in.

The inside-out approach involves starting with the activities of the company and matching them up with the overall issues of society. For example, if a company runs manufacturing plants in various cities, it could consider what impact the plants might be having on the local environments, such as air or water pollution and consider strategies to reduce any negative impact. Or they could look at the role they are playing in the community and perhaps sponsor local team sports for the benefit of everyone living in the area.

The outside-in approach involves observing and thinking about the environment and how it affects the company. This could include the legal environment and how friendly it is to business activities. Or it could look at whether the local environment provides enough skilled workers. Perhaps the company would adopt training programs to help address deficiencies or sponsor programs at a local community college.

Adidas modified its manufacturing process to reduce the amount of plastic in the oceans. They did this by partnering and modifying its core product without altering its business model. It might even enhance their product marketability in the eyes of the growing numbers of customers having concerns about the environment.

Determine Priorities

Prioritizing objectives enables the company to develop practical action plans. Integrated thinking is needed in this process so that the concerns of society and the financial needs of the company both can be taken into account.

Materiality constitutes an important part of determining priorities. A company must perform a materiality assessment to identify the most significant social, environmental, and governance impacts of its business. This helps prioritize CSR initiatives and allocate resources effectively. Conducting a materiality assessment helps identify the issues that are most relevant to the company and its stakeholders. This assessment considers both internal and external perspectives to determine the key social, environmental, and governance aspects that have the most significant impact on the company's operations, reputation, and value chain. The company might consider conducting a stakeholder engagement exercise or utilizing industry-specific sustainability frameworks to support its assessment of priorities.

Set Specific Goals and Targets

Once the material issues are identified, the next step is to set measurable goals and targets. By setting clear objectives, companies can track their progress, demonstrate commitment, and continuously strive for improvement in their CSR initiatives. They can also use these objectives in developing comprehensive CSR policies and programs that address the identified material issues. Strategic CSR requires embedding CSR considerations throughout the company's operations. Integrating CSR considerations into all levels of the organization and across business functions involves training employees on CSR principles, promoting responsible decision making, and embedding sustainability practices into day-to-day operations. It includes integrating social and environmental criteria into procurement practices, supply chain management, product development, and employee practices. For example, companies can adopt sustainable sourcing practices, develop eco-friendly products, and promote diversity and inclusion in their workforce. By integrating CSR into the core business functions, companies create long-term value while addressing societal and environmental challenges. They should ensure that the policies are aligned with legal requirements, industry standards, and international guidelines. Encourage innovation and collaboration to identify opportunities for positive impact.

Managing a CSR system is an ongoing process that requires commitment, adaptability, and a genuine desire to make a positive impact. By integrating CSR into the core business strategy, companies can contribute to a sustainable future while enhancing their reputation and long-term success.

Collaborate and Engage With Stakeholders

Stakeholder engagement is crucial in implementing strategic CSR. Companies need to understand the expectations and concerns of their stakeholders, including employees, customers, suppliers, communities, and investors. By engaging stakeholders in dialogue, involving them in decision-making processes, and soliciting their feedback, companies can gain valuable insights, build trust, and ensure that their CSR initiatives are aligned with stakeholder expectations.

Employees play a pivotal role in driving CSR initiatives. To foster a culture of social responsibility, companies can implement employee engagement programs. These programs can include volunteering opportunities, skills-based pro bono projects, and sustainability training. By empowering employees to contribute to social and environmental initiatives, companies not only enhance their CSR impact but also improve employee morale, satisfaction, and retention.

Addressing complex social and environmental challenges requires collaboration. Companies can form partnerships with nongovernmental organizations (NGOs), academic institutions, government agencies, and other businesses to pool resources, expertise, and networks. Collaborative initiatives can amplify the impact of CSR efforts, drive innovation, and promote shared learning and best practices.

Develop and Launch Action Plans

Too many strategic planning exercises end up as reports sitting on a dusty shelf; the most common reason for this is that they did not contain workable action plans or perhaps did not contain action plans at all. Also, buy-in (including active participation and motivation) is absolutely essential in order for the plans to work out. This includes buy-in from the people to be given the responsibility to carry out the plans and buy-in from the management, who must ultimately take responsibility for the outcomes from a corporate perspective. This may require organizational changes to bring the right resources to the new tasks.

It is also important for the action plans to include specific targets that can be measured and enable progress to be monitored.

Measure, Monitor, and Evaluate

The results of a CSR program must be monitored regularly and measured against the overall objectives previously established. A steering committee is useful for making this work effectively.

The steering committee can regularly review and evaluate the effectiveness of the CSR system and initiatives, seek feedback from stakeholders, conduct internal audits, and stay updated on emerging trends and best practices.

Tracking and measuring the progress of CSR initiatives involves establishing key performance indicators (KPIs) and metrics. The committee can then monitor and report on the company's performance against these metrics on a regular basis. This data will help identify areas for improvement and demonstrate the company's commitment to CSR.

The assessment and evaluation process also necessarily includes the social and environmental impacts of the supply chain. The company must encourage suppliers to adhere to ethical practices, such as fair labor standards and responsible sourcing. Implement supplier codes of conduct and conduct audits and due diligence programs to assess compliance.

To ensure the effectiveness of CSR initiatives, companies need to establish robust monitoring and evaluation systems. Measuring the outcomes and impacts of CSR efforts against set goals enables companies to track progress and identify areas for improvement. Regular reporting of CSR performance enhances transparency and accountability, fostering trust among stakeholders and showcasing the company's commitment to sustainability.

Measuring CSR

Operating a CSR policy over the longer term requires that there be useful and specific reporting to stakeholders and within layers of management. Many of the goals in CSR are "soft," and therefore difficult to measure, but transparency is important, so in the process of developing goals, it is necessary to find or develop useful metrics to use. The best source of specific metrics developed for use with sustainability reporting and, therefore, useful for much of CSR reporting is published by the GRI and

SASB. Some of them are already devised for particular industries and others are available for more general application.

Most companies that report on sustainability use metrics to reflect their performance in the areas of interest. Common ones, for example, revolve around gas emissions. For example, the SEC has announced new disclosure rules that would require listed companies to not only disclose risks that are "reasonably likely to have a material impact on their business, results of operations, or financial condition," but also to disclose information about its direct greenhouse gas (GHG) emissions (Scope 1) and indirect emissions (Scope 2).

The World Economic Forum (WEF) has released numerous metrics that have been widely adopted. According to the WEF website, under their Stakeholder Metrics Initiative, over 130 companies implement sustainability reporting metrics.[†]

The metrics of the WEF are presented in their publication "Measuring Stakeholder Capitalism Towards Common Metrics and Consistent Reporting of Sustainable Value Creation," published in September 2020. The metrics are presented under four categories: governance, planet, people, and prosperity. For example, the metrics under governance include measures regarding governing purpose, quality of governing body, shareholder engagement, ethical behavior, risk, and opportunity oversight. Other metrics will develop as companies gain further experience with sustainability reporting and CSR.

Communicate and Market the New Initiative

Communicate CSR initiatives and progress transparently through various channels such as annual sustainability reports, website content, and social media platforms. Share successes, challenges, and lessons learned to maintain accountability and engage stakeholders.

[†] See www.weforum.org/impact/stakeholder-capitalism-reporting-metrics-davos2023/.

A good CSR program creates a marketing opportunity. One that will not only lead to increased revenues but will serve to improve the reputation of the company.

Maple Leaf Mills does a good job of this. It is important to note that the social purpose of Maple Leaf Mills is closely related to its core products and its business model. Integration of its social purposes and its financial business model comes more naturally and is much more feasible than if it had defined a high-end, vague social policy and then tried to figure out how to fit it into its business model. They get into more specifics on their website; for example, "high-quality meat products, meat that's never been treated with antibiotics and plant-based protein options" are mentioned.

Adopt Continuous Improvement Techniques

Implementing strategic CSR is an ongoing process. Companies must regularly review and revise their CSR strategy to adapt to evolving social and environmental trends, emerging issues, and stakeholder expectations. Learning from experiences, both successes and challenges, allows companies to refine their CSR approach and align it with changing circumstances. Continuous improvement then becomes a part of the management of CSR. Adapt and refine the CSR strategy accordingly to ensure continuous improvement and relevance.

ISO 26000

A useful aid in the adoption of strategic CSR can also be found in ISO 26000, which deals with the broad area of social responsibility for all organizations, including small and medium-sized organizations. Thus, although it does not specifically refer to corporate social responsibility, it nevertheless can be applied to it.

The introduction in the ISO 26000 document states its objective as follows:

"Organizations around the world, and their stakeholders, are becoming increasingly aware of the need for, and benefits of, socially responsible behaviour. The objective of social responsibility is to contribute to sustainable development."

The ISO 26000 document describes the important factors and conditions that have influenced the development of social responsibility and that continue to affect its nature and practice. It also describes the concept of social responsibility itself—what it means and how it applies to organizations.

It addresses two aspects of social responsibility: an organization's recognition of its social responsibility and its identification of, and engagement with, its stakeholders. It provides guidance on putting social responsibility into practice in an organization including:

1. Understanding the social responsibility of an organization;
2. Making social responsibility integral to its policies, organizational culture, strategies, and operations;
3. Making social responsibility integral to its policies, organizational culture, strategies, and operations;
4. Building internal competency for social responsibility;
5. Undertaking internal and external communication on social responsibility; and
6. Regularly reviewing these actions and practices related to social responsibility.

ISO 26000 is not a certifiable standard but rather a guidance document. And it does offer some useful guidance in implementing CSR.

Strategic Planning for CSR

In this chapter, we have reviewed various techniques that can be used for CSR strategic planning. Strategic CSR is intended to be an ongoing strategy in an organization. Therefore, as an organization reviews its strategy on a continuing basis, its CSR strategy would be included in this review and over time, it should evolve with the emerging needs of the organization and its stakeholders.

CHAPTER 9

How to Establish Effective Controls Over Sustainability Information

Internal controls have long been a requirement for protecting and preserving the integrity and quality of business information. Initially, their chief application was for numerical financial information, but gradually, they increased in scope to include narrative information because there is a lot of narrative in financial reporting, particularly in notes to the financial statements and documents like the MD&A.

In recent years, large companies listed with the SEC have been required to report on the controls in place over their financial reporting process. They are also required to obtain an audit opinion on these controls. And so the idea of controls over financial reporting has become a very important element of an internal control framework.

With the advent of assurance on sustainability information, good internal controls are essential to the provision of high-quality, reliable information. Therefore, it is essential for companies to implement a good system of internal controls over the accumulation and reporting of sustainability information. Moreover, with the release of the S1 and S2 standards of the International Sustainability Standards Board, the focus is on sustainability issues that are most likely to affect the financial position of the company. Such disclosures are to be made in the annual reports in conjunction with the financial reports, making the sustainability disclosures an extension of the financial disclosures on which there have long been audit reports given. The expectation is that the control systems supporting the financial reports and those supporting the sustainability disclosures will ultimately become the same systems.

Traditionally, internal controls over financial reporting have been managed in the finance area of the companies. In the past, sustainability reporting has largely been organized under the PR and admin areas of the company. However, with regulatory requirements for audited sustainability information, such as those of the SEC, and the advent of integrated reporting, companies wanting to develop good reliable sustainability information have been looking to bring together the various departments to capitalize on the established expertise that finance has built in developing and administering relevant internal controls. The most common set of standards used for establishing and reporting on internal controls is that of the Committee of Sponsoring Organizations of the Treadway Commission (COSO), which published its Internal Control—Integrated Framework (the Framework) in 1992 to provide guidance on the controls appropriate for (mostly) financial reporting. It was then updated and expanded in 2013 to include certain guiding principles.

In the 2013 expansion, the committee said "The Framework has been enhanced by expanding the financial reporting category of objectives to include other important forms of reporting, such as non-financial and internal reporting." In the view of many people, this reference to non-financial opened the door for sustainability reporting.

The COSO framework sets out internal control objectives in three categories:

1. **Operations** objectives, which include performance goals and security over company assets and focus on the effectiveness and efficiency of business operations.
2. **Reporting** objectives, which are related to both internal and external financial and nonfinancial reporting and focus on transparency, timeliness, and reliability of the organization's reporting processes.
3. **Compliance** objectives, which focus on adherence to laws and regulations with which the organization must comply.

The framework sets out five components to an internal control system, which are as follows:

1. **Control environment:** The "set of standards, processes, and structures that provide the basis for carrying out internal controls across

the organization." This component includes ethical values, organizational structure, commitment to employing competent employees, and human resources policies.

2. **Risk assessment:** The organization's analysis of the risks posed by internal and external changes, the ability to establish suitable objectives for the business, and the process for weighing perceived risks against risk tolerances.

3. **Control activities:** The tasks and activities involved in operating the internal controls, including actions such as "authorizations, verifications, reconciliations, and business performance reviews."

4. **Information and communication:** Relevant and high-quality information to control functions. These include internal messages emphasizing the importance of control responsibilities and external messages providing clear communication of expectations with external parties.

5. **Monitoring**: Ongoing evaluations of internal controls built into business processes as well as regular separate evaluations, which will vary based on the level of risk, system effectiveness, and regulatory requirements.

Application of COSO to Sustainability Reporting

For several years, a great many companies have produced sustainability reports. In those reports, companies provide information on the impact their activities are having on the environment and the steps they are taking to reduce their negative impact. Such mitigative activities as reforestation, carbon emissions control, and water discharge control are often featured. The negative impacts are often downplayed or not mentioned.

In more recent standards, the emphasis has shifted to the idea of value creation. For example, "The SASB defines sustainability in the broader context of an organization's capacity and capability for longer-term value creation across a variety of dimensions, including:

- Environment
- Social capital
- Human capital
- Business model and innovation
- Leadership and governance"[1]

As can be seen, not only did modern standards shift to value creation, SASB also expanded the scope of sustainability reporting to include human capital separately and the business model and innovation idea. Arguably, these additional items would have been included in ESG anyway; the SASB standards do add additional focus on them.

When one applies COSO to sustainability reporting, recognizing that COSO has largely been used for financial reporting, it is necessary to consider how sustainability reporting differs from financial reporting. There are several differences. Here are a few:

1. The subject matter of the two types of reporting is very different. Financial reporting centers around the traditional financial statements and measures of financial operating results and financial position. Sustainability reporting includes the type of reporting mentioned earlier—environmental matters and so on.

2. Financial reporting has been the core of reporting to investors and creditors for centuries. Sustainability reporting has existed only for a few decades and has not traditionally been directed primarily to investors. Because of this, financial reporting tends to be more structured and standardized, although even within that structure and regulatory requirements, companies do have some latitude in how information is presented in terms of what would be meaningful for users.

3. Financial reporting is primarily numbers based, although the amount of text included in it has grown tremendously in recent years. Sustainability reporting has been largely qualitative text with the use of some quantitative metrics. The new emerging standards encourage the use of more metrics.

4. Financial reporting includes some future-oriented information. Sustainability reporting often includes much more.

5. Financial information is generated from relatively closed and well-established systems with built in controls. Sustainability information comes from a variety of sources, often with little or no controls built in.

In applying COSO to sustainability reporting, all the COSO objectives would apply. The five components would need to be addressed in the context of the sustainability information streams, which would need to be identified and documented.

The *control environment* can be evaluated by reviewing the ethical values, organizational structure, commitment to employing competent employees, and human resources policies. Since the control environment for sustainability is not as well established and rigorous, areas for enhancement should be identified and acted upon. *Risk assessment* involves identifying what the risks are and what the tolerance for misstatement would be for the company. In financial reporting, materiality plays an important role in assessing potential misstatements. Relatively concrete guidelines exist for measuring materiality, such as the percentage of net income. For sustainability reporting, because the information is largely nonnumerical, such guidelines are not available. However, the general definition of materiality has always been based on the idea that any misstatement is material if it is likely to influence the decisions of the readers. That same basis applies to sustainability. But the measurement is more judgmental.

It is in the area of *control activities* where the most active change needs to take place to apply COSO to sustainability reporting. Such actions as "authorizations, verifications, reconciliations, and business performance reviews" would need to be specifically applied to the identified sustainability information streams. In addition, under the *information and communication* category, relevant and high-quality information would be directed to control functions, including internal messages emphasizing the importance of control responsibilities and external messages providing clear communication of expectations with external parties. As with financial controls, monitoring, including evaluations of internal controls built into business processes, is critical for ongoing effectiveness of controls.

Application of COSO to Integrated Reporting

"An integrated report is a concise communication about how an organization's strategy, governance, performance and prospects, in the context of its external environment, lead to the creation of value in the short, medium and long term."[2]

When reporting evolves into integrated reporting, the integration of finance and the relevant nonfinancial areas will be more complete.

Essentially, the concept of integrated thinking will, if successfully implemented, strive to ensure that all efforts of an organization to create value will be taken into account in reporting, not just financial value. The new ISSB standards, with the requirement that sustainability information be disclosed with the financial statements, are, in effect, a step in the direction of a form of integrated reporting.

Introduction of integrated reporting adds additional focus to applying COSO to financial and sustainability reporting processes because the two sets of processes would be expected to become much more integrated through the implementation of integrated thinking, which involves considering all activities of the company in terms of how they impact the sustainability as well as financial welfare of the company. For example, if a company establishes a factory on the shore of a bay, then it would report on the costs of establishing and running the new facility as well as its financial results, but it would also report on the impact of the new factory on the atmosphere, the water and the soil. They would report on such matters as ocean levels and their expected impact on the factory, as this is indeed the essence of sustainability. No more would they report on the financial impacts in one place and the other impacts in another report located someplace else.

The idea of combining controls and information flows on an integrated basis poses new issues. The objectives of the controls would be restructured to reflect all the various value indicators. But the implementation of controls is always influenced by the nature of the information flows being managed. As previously noted, the information flows for sustainability information tend to be much more often in narrative form than financial information flows. This poses a problem in that narrative is notoriously difficult to work with and is often biased.

Many people feel that bringing together these flows would be expedited by having them done on a structured basis, such as by using XBRL.

At the reporting level, the US Securities and Exchange Commission (SEC) recently provided support for this idea. "At a recent open meeting, the (SEC) put forward landmark new rules on mandatory climate-related disclosures, in proposals described by Chair Gary Gensler as 'driven by the needs of investors and issuers.'" XBRL US noted that "we are pleased to see that (as expected) these new disclosures would need to be tagged in a structured, machine-readable data language—namely Inline XBRL." The digital tagging requirement would extend not only to quantitative facts but also to narrative disclosures.[3]

"A study by EY found that two-thirds of global investors evaluate non-financial disclosures. However, only half of this group uses a structured process to make their assessments."[4] With integrated reporting, it is much more feasible to use structured techniques.

There is much work to be done before the use of XBRL can be a reality for disclosures on an integrated basis. Taxonomies exist for financial reporting and some sustainability reporting. But there are none that are fully integrated. Ad hoc solutions are possible, but comparability and quality require that the taxonomies be developed through rigorous programs by recognized bodies. The SEC and FASB need to work together as do EFRAG, ISSB, and others for Europe. Other parts of the world have similar issues. So the road to full integration of structured data may be a long one.

In the meantime, COSO is adaptable to controls over integrated reporting because it has long been used for financial and nonfinancial reporting and, as a working vehicle for establishing and monitoring controls, should stand up very well. It's also a structure that lends itself to applications other than financial since the general principles can apply to many types of operational controls.

Assurance

Strong internal control is a necessary element of any system to support sustainability reporting, integrated reporting, and strategic CSR. There have been growing calls for independent assurance to be provided on sustainability and integrated reports. This will encourage compliance with accepted standards of disclosure, such as those of the ISSB and GRI, to improve the quality and accuracy of disclosures and reduce and hopefully eliminate greenwashing.

With the recent, rapid changes taking place, corporate reporting, which was once focused on financial reporting, is now in the process of incorporating sustainability reporting. While companies had long reported on sustainability, it was focused on informing the general public rather than primarily on investors and their needs. A cynic would say it was often focused on public relations. The move to reporting on sustainability matters of concern to investors was a major shift and was supported by regulators such as the SEC. This is likely to lead to the next step—integrated reporting and assurance thereon.

Given the different scenarios in which sustainability reporting can take place, then various types of assurance would apply.

At present, the different types of assurance generally recognized include the following:

1. Reasonable assurance, culminating in an opinion as to whether a report presents the subject matter fairly in accordance with certain defined criteria. There must be criteria, which in audit reports on financial statements are generally accepted as accounting principles;
2. Limited assurance, culminating in a conclusion that the author has conducted a review and has no reason to believe that the subject of the report does not conform to the designated criteria;
3. Assurance engagements other than audits or reviews of financial statements and other historical financial information (such as audits and reviews of nonfinancial information);
4. Related services engagements (such as an engagement to report on supplementary matters to a third party, a compilation engagement, or an agreed-upon procedures engagement); and
5. Reports on internal controls over the reporting process.

The types of sustainability reporting that have a bearing on the style of assurance that might be provided are as follows:

1. Separate sustainability reports presented in accordance with standards such as the GRI standards;
2. Financial reports that include sustainability metrics and disclosures in accordance with standards such as those of the ISSB; and
3. Integrated reports presented in accordance with the standards of the integrated International Reporting Framework originally developed by the International Integrated Reporting Council, now under the responsibility of the IFRS Foundation.

The International Assurance Standards that are most applicable to sustainability reports are the pending ISSB 5000, ISAE Section 3000, and attestation engagements other than audits or reviews of historical financial information. Section 3000 specifically mentions sustainability reports. Where sustainability is required to be included in the financial statements, then the audit standards of the IAASB must be followed.

ISSB 5000 is the most important document for assurance engagements on sustainability reports. It covers limited assurance engagements and reasonable assurance engagements. It would be applied for assurance of sustainability information that is not required to be included in the audited financial statements.

CHAPTER 10

Summary and Conclusions

The Pressures

We have seen that the development of corporate social responsibility must originate at some point from a social consciousness, either from within the company or from outside. Most often, the consciousness comes from outside. Companies are being pressured by all their stakeholders, including investors, creditors, employees, customers, suppliers, communities, the general public, and more. Companies must be accountable to their stakeholders, and there is much evidence that the most profitable and successful companies pay attention to their stakeholder needs and concerns in order to sustain and grow their business.

The focus of the pressure is quite broad. Too often people assume that sustainability means climate-related matters; however, the concerns of stakeholders are much broader than that. They include climate of course, but also human rights are high on their list, including not only the treatment of people within the company but also in their extended supply chains. They also include questions of diversity and ethics. In general they include social and governmental as well as environmental matters.

In current times, the pressures on companies for change are considerable and show no signs of abating.

The History

It's not the first time in history that companies have been subjected to demands beyond the making of money. Nobody knows when it first started, but we have traced the history from the times of the Roman Republic, which was when numerous companies similar to modern corporations were formed. The companies were formed to serve the needs of the state, including the mounting and financing of the armies they needed at the time. This was a few hundred years before the emergence of the Roman Empire. Similar demands persisted during the Italian Renaissance when corporations were formed to serve the interests of the state, the church, and rich families such as the Medicis. It was recognized that the companies needed to make good profits in order to discharge their purposes. A focus on profit as a goal in itself is a fairly recent phenomenon, marked by the formation of companies such as the Ford Motor Company and the multinationals, augmented by the pronouncements of economists such as Milton Friedman, who famously stated that profit is the sole goal of companies. But recently, there has been increased questioning of the role of profit and growth and of globalization itself.

Instead, there is a growing awareness, perhaps because of the spread of technology and information about global conditions, that companies need to help alleviate, or at least not contribute to, the threats and injustices in the world. This is a major reason why companies are being asked to take responsibility for their supply chains, which have extended to many parts of the world as a result of globalization. For many modern consumers, especially millennials, the practices of entering into the production of the products they buy are very important. If they find that shoes, for example, are being manufactured by children in slave labor conditions, they will be inclined not to buy them. As a result, companies need to conduct due diligence on their supply chains to determine that such processes are not happening.

Many companies have responded to these pressures by adopting policies, in addition to due diligence for supply chains, diversity in governance, reduction of emissions, and other sustainability measures. Many have also responded by producing sustainability reports. And professional organizations have begun to step up with standards to add rigor and consistency to such reporting.

Sustainability Reporting

During 2023, the ISSB released its first two standards, which constituted a considerable advance in reporting to shareholders and other stakeholders interested in financial and business reporting. However, the release also solidified the division in sustainability reporting because the standards focused on finance and business-related sustainability matters. This is in contrast to the well-established process of reporting, generally in accordance with the GRI standards, to a broader range of stakeholders on a broader range of sustainability matters of interest. In effect, the ISSB addressed a subset of sustainability issues.

Exactly how this works out in the long term remains to be seen. It will lead to better financial reporting since the risks and opportunities presented by sustainability issues relevant to financial and business concerns will be disclosed to shareholders, which will help them in their decision making. On the other hand, the standards at present only loosely define the word sustainability, which is likely to lead to inconsistencies in the types of issues disclosed. Future standards will have to deal quickly with these inconsistencies. The different definitions of sustainability will also continue to confuse report users.

When sustainability reporting primarily to shareholders became formalized, the idea gained traction that it would make sense to integrate sustainability reporting with the long-established financial reporting. Integrated reporting was adopted by some companies. This was a significant task involving a wide range of personnel in the company. It was found by many that the established experience and training of those involved in financial reporting could assist with stabilizing and formalizing the resultant integrated reporting process.

Integrated Reporting

Integrated reporting differs from the other styles of reporting because it is based on the creation of value in the six capitals (*financial, manufactured, intellectual, human, social and relationship,* and *natural*) used by an enterprise. This identification of capitals helps to clarify what is meant by sustainability, as the capitals include, in addition to financial, the other five, which are more identifiable with traditional concepts of sustainability, particularly the human, social and relationship, and natural capitals. As a result, the disclosures under integrated reporting are more likely to include a broad range of sustainability issues than would the ISSB disclosures, as presently defined.

Integrated Thinking

To enable the company to properly prepare integrated reports, it was clear that there needed to be a shift in organizational thinking toward integrated thinking, which would bring to bear into the reporting process the knowledge of all those with the expertise and experience in both financial and sustainability issues. Integrated thinking is a work in progress with many companies. The Integrated Reporting Foundation itself characterized it as a long-term goal.

The degree of change required to implement integrated thinking varies among companies, depending upon how integrated they already were and how they have made decisions in the past. For some, it would require a simple change in procedure, perhaps some joint meetings of different facets of the organization. For others it would require reallocation of duties in some areas, to ensure that different points of view were taken into account. For other companies, it might require a full-scale reorganization, involving the shuffling of departments and their responsibilities and assigning new personnel to work together.

A significant opportunity for companies and society then presents itself. If companies begin to integrate their thinking in order to prepare integrated reports, they can alter their strategic objectives to integrate all aspects of the functions of the company, thus improving their overall relationship with society. Some companies implementing integrated thinking would do this anyway. However, others would not. This raises the idea of corporate social responsibility (CSR), on which there is a long history and extensive literature to assist companies in moving in that direction from a strategic point of view.

Strategic Corporate Social Responsibility

Strategic CSR extends beyond but incorporates integrated thinking; it directs its objectives by accomplishing better corporate reporting and also better management overall of the company by earning profits in the "right" way. We have emphasized that CSR does not conflict with profit making but rather augments it and perhaps even enhances it. It is an opportunity that no corporation should ignore and that society cannot let the companies ignore.

Adoption of CSR involves another shift in thinking and a significant move beyond the idea of corporate reporting to embrace strategic and operational modifications. It does not involve a move away from focus on profits but rather a shift to focus on how the money is made. For example, if profits are made at the expense of disadvantaged groups in society, then this would be addressed by the company. There are several companies that have done this, including Maple Leaf Foods and BMW. It created a major marketing opportunity, and the response of the public and customers has been very positive.

Corporations can move into the future in many different ways. How much control they have over their future depends on the way they choose. They can move ahead by being nudged and prompted by their environment, by the legal system and by their stakeholders, as has been the case for much of history. Or they can seize the moment and develop strategies that work best for them in the long term, by maintaining control over their destiny.

The world is changing very quickly and we do not know how quickly or the direction it will take. What we do know is that massive change is a reality and that much of the change will be driven by climate change. Whether climate change is caused by humans is not entirely relevant. Nor is the fact that some of the extremes we see happening have happened before, say 100 or 1,000 years ago, or even many millennia ago. The fact that extreme climate is upon us and that it will cause many thousands (millions?) of deaths during our lifetimes is what should concern us. As should the fact that science is telling us that there are steps we can take to mitigate the problem. We all have a responsibility to help in any way we can.

That is the essence of corporate social responsibility. The corporations have the opportunity and the resources to help, all while doing what their business model demands for the benefit of their stakeholders, their shareholders, and society generally. What's the problem in making the decision to follow this course? How could any other decision make any sense?

Appendix A—Analysis of a Prominent Sustainability Report

As stated on its website, GF (Georg Fischer Ltd) of Switzerland has three divisions—GF Piping Systems, GF Casting Solutions, and GF Machining Solutions—that offer products and solutions to enable the safe transport of liquids and gases, as well as lightweight casting components and high-precision manufacturing technologies. As a sustainability and innovation leader, GF strives to achieve profitable growth while having offered superior value to its customers for more than 200 years. Founded in 1802, the Corporation is headquartered in Switzerland.

This example sustainability report was published by GF in 2022. It is available at https://georgfischer.com. Any quotes below are from this website.

Commentary

To provide a focus for its sustainability strategy, GF established a Sustainability Framework 2025, which consists of three focus areas. These include:

1. Product Innovation—to "focus on innovating products and solutions for a sustainable lifecycle."
2. Climate and Resources—to "decouple resource consumption from growth in its operations and supply chain, thereby minimizing its environmental footprint."
3. Diversity and Inclusion—to "foster a diverse, engaging, and safe workplace and strive to be the best employer it can be."

The company reported that products with social or environmental benefits in 2021 generated 60 percent of sales, up from 58 percent in the preceding year. Greenhouse gas (GHG) emissions fell 17 percent compared to the base year of 2019. Waste sent to landfill or incineration fell 9 percent compared to a baseline average of the previous three years.

This process of setting specific goals and then reporting on progress toward meeting them is an important part of good reporting. The goals are specific and measurable and the appropriate metrics appear in the report.

One innovation in their program for 2021 was to monitor sustainability levels within their supply chain. To benchmark this program, the company issued a Code for Sustainability to their business partners and then began a monitoring process to see how well it was being followed. During 2021, they met their goal of checking 16 percent of their procurement spending. The company also communicates their sustainability objectives with their supply chain through inclusion of the code in its contracts, webinars, and updates.

In another new metric pertaining to diversity and inclusion, the company exceeded its target of including "25 percent women among new management appointments, with 30 percent of newly appointed managers in 2021 being women."

An important part of the report is the inclusion of detailed and extensive tables of metrics. For example, the table on *Environmental Performance Indicators* includes metrics on energy consumption, GHG and air emissions, water and wastewater, waste and recycling, and other similar items. The table on social performance indicators includes data on employees, diversity according to gender and age, training and professional development, health and safety, and community.

Overall, the report provides an excellent view of a company committed to environmental and social concerns.

Appendix B—Analysis of an Integrated Report

ABN AMRO is one of the Netherlands' leading banks. It has a focus on Northwest Europe, providing banking services to retail, private, and business clients. With more than 19,000 employees worldwide, their vision is to be a personal bank in the digital age.

The bank issued this integrated report, which is available at https://www.abnamro.com/annualreport.

A section of the report explains how the bank creates value. It refers to the six capitals of the IR Framework and places greatest emphasis on the financial, social, and environmental, "applying strict rules on lending and investment activities, increasing financing for sustainable business, and encouraging employees to speak out if they suspect any violation of our standards or guidelines."

The report goes on to provide some metrics regarding the inputs and outputs for each of the capitals. The explanation of the social capital stresses client relationships, employee engagement and motivation, and industry networks and cooperation. Later, there is a discussion of diversity, skills development, salaries, and wages. The environmental (natural) aspect was explained as consumption of energy, water, and other natural resources at their offices.

Finally, the report concludes with sections on financial results, governance, assurance, and other explanations of their reporting process.

Appendix C—Example of a Company Following Strategic CSR

Mountain Equipment Co-op (MEC) is a Canadian consumers' cooperative based in Vancouver, BC, Canada, with 2,500 employees that sells outdoor recreational gear and clothing through 22 retail stores across Canada and its website at https://www.mec.ca.

MEC states its social purpose as "to inspire and enable everyone to lead active outdoor lifestyles." The company accomplishes this not only by selling outdoor gear and clothing but also by matching customers with gear that suits their needs, offering activity events such as races, meet-ups and classes, embedding their principles in their products, and advocating for conservation and physical activity. They are dedicated to bringing about a future where Canadians of all ages are inspired to live healthy outdoor lifestyles, make good use of Canada's parks, wilderness, and outdoor recreation areas and have a strong connection to nature. MEC wishes to inspire other organizations and individuals to adopt ESG values.

To reduce barriers to outdoor activity, MEC often arranges and funds partnerships such as "Parkbus," a MEC-funded social enterprise. Parkbus operates bus services to National and Provincial Parks from major cities across Canada free of cost. By offering sustainable, equal access to nature through collective transportation, MEC helps more people can appreciate the outdoors.

Besides providing funding, MEC also provides their partners with donated products, employee volunteers, and opportunities to get in front of their five million members.

MEC is also a social innovator. The company was a founding member of the Sustainable Apparel Coalition (SAC), which was launched in 2011 as the clothing and footwear industry's alliance for more sustainable production. SAC's vision is that the industry creates no unnecessary environmental harm and has a positive impact on people and communities. The coalition has developed the Higg Index, which is a suite of tools to measure environmental and social impacts of brands, retailers, manufacturers, factories, and products. As an active member of SAC, MEC has been helping to create these industry tools and formalize a standardized way to communicate social and environmental impacts of products to consumers.

Another social innovation championed by MEC addresses ocean pollution. MEC was one of the first clothing businesses to fund research into apparel-linked micro-fiber pollution in aquatic environments. It is trying to determine the rate of fiber loss from home laundering that ends up in oceans through laundry water. This understanding is key to re-engineer fabrics to reduce micro-fiber pollution. MEC has funded micro-fiber research by drawing on the expertise and technical capacity of the Ocean Wise Plastics Lab.

In MEC's experience, defining your social purpose is a journey that must be bought into from top to bottom and must be integrated into the way business is done. MEC has used its purpose as a true guide.

MEC has a responsible sourcing policy, covering its own labeled products as well as products they sell from other brands. Under their responsible sourcing, MEC has developed a code of conduct for the factories working in their supply chain and takes steps to ensure that they comply with the code, operate according to their values, manage risks, comply with the law, and maintain good relationships with other businesses and suppliers. Regular audits are undertaken to ensure that the suppliers are upholding these standards.

Various major initiatives were taken on by MEC in the field of social and environmental responsibility. In terms of products, the company committed to using 100 percent organic cotton for all MEC-branded apparel and set yearly targets to increase its offering of products made from recycled materials. In December 2007, MEC became the first retailer in Canada to stop selling water bottles and food containers containing a chemical that is used to make some plastics that have been linked to increased incidence of cancer and other diseases. In 2008, MEC eliminated all single-use shopping bags from its stores. In 2019, 88 percent of MEC apparel and sleeping bag materials were bluesign certified.

Bluesign is a third-party environmental, health, and safety standard for the textiles industry.

Social initiatives include the promotion of a variety of outdoor education opportunities to its members through an online calendar of events. In 2010, MEC launched a new green building initiative, the aim of which was to ensure that MEC would be leaders in building and operating environmentally friendly facilities. Its Winnipeg, Montreal, and Ottawa stores also comply with C2000 standards Advanced Commercial Buildings Program.

And in March 2018, MEC announced that it would no longer stock products made by Vista Outdoor, in the wake of the Stoneman Douglas High School shooting, because some of Vista Outdoor's profits are derived from the production of assault weapons.

This is a remarkable set of initiatives for a single company, showing a commitment to sustainability and the ability to align the initiatives with other profit-oriented objectives and strategies of the organization.

Notes

Chapter 2

1. Wall Street (1987).
2. The Rise of the Social Pillar: An Introduction to the "S" in ESG (n.d.), p. 4.

Chapter 3

1. Magnuson (2022).
2. Op cit (n.d.), p. 67.
3. Op cit (n.d.), p. 70.
4. Op cit (n.d.), p. 99
5. Op cit (n.d.), p. 100.
6. Op cit (n.d.)
7. Op cit (n.d.), p. 178.
8. Op cit (n.d.), p. 167.
9. Wickert and Risi (2019).
10. Op cit (n.d.), p. 214.
11. Op cit (n.d.), p. 253.

Chapter 4

1. McKinsey & Co (2013)
2. GRI Foundation Document (n.d.), p. 9.

Chapter 5

1. Integrated reporting framework (n.d.), p. 53.
2. The future of Corporate Reporting—Creating the Dynamics for Change (2016).
3. Ibid, p. 17.
4. Integrated thinking principles (2022).

Chapter 6

1. Chandler (n.d.), pp. 184–185.
2. Wickert and Risi (n.d.), p. 8.
3. Wickert and Risi (2019), p. 6.

Chapter 7

1. Chandler (2023).
2. Wickert and Risi (2019).
3. Wickert and Risi (n.d.), p. 86.
4. Schwartz and Carroll (2003), p. 512.
5. Chandler (n.d.), p. 15.
6. Chandler (n.d.), p. 23.
7. Chandler (n.d.), p 38.
8. Wickert and Risi (2019), p. 16.
9. Chandler (n.d.), p. 69.
10. Chandler (n.d.), p. 28.
11. Chandler (n.d.), p. 36.
12. Chandler (n.d.), p. 43.
13. Corel Strandberg (2020), p. 11.

References

"Building a Human Firewall to Block Cyberattacks: Lessons From SoSafe." April 10, 2013. McKinsey & Co. www.mckinsey.com/capabilities/mckinsey-digital/our-insights/building-a-human-firewall-to-block-cyberattacks-lessons-from-sosafe.

Chandler, D. 2023. *Strategic Corporate Social Responsibility—Sustainable Value Creation*. 6th ed. Sage Publishing.

Chandler, D. n.d. p. 23.

Chandler, D. n.d. p. 28.

Chandler, D. n.d. p. 36.

Chandler, D. n.d. p. 38.

Chandler, D. n.d. p. 43.

Chandler, D. n.d. *Strategic Corporate Social Responsibility*, 15. SAGE Publications. Kindle Edition.

Chandler, D. n.d. *Strategic Corporate Social Responsibility*, 184–185. SAGE Publications. Kindle Edition.

Chandler, D. n.d. *Strategic Corporate Social Responsibility*, 69. SAGE Publications. Kindle Edition.

Corel Strandberg. January 2020. "Best CSR Practices in Canada—Case Studies." p. 11. Strandberg Consulting.

Corporate Social Responsibility, Cambridge Elements, Christopher Wickert and David Risi, Cambridge University Press, July 2019.

GRI Foundation Document. n.d. p. 9.

Ibid. p. 17.

Integrated Reporting Framework. n.d. p. 53.

Integrated Thinking Principles. 2022. Value Reporting Foundation. www.integrated reporting.org/integrated-thinking-principles-download/.

Magnuson, W. November 2022. *For Profit: A History of Corporations*. New York, NY: Basic Books.

Op cit. n.d.

Op cit. n.d. p. 167.

Op cit. n.d. p. 178.

Op cit. n.d. p. 214.

Op cit. n.d. p. 253.

Op cit. n.d. p. 67.

Op cit. n.d. p. 100.

Op cit. n.d. p. 70.

Op cit. n.d. p. 99.

Schwartz, M.S. and A.B. Carroll. 2003. "Corporate Social Responsibility: A Three-domain Approach." *Business Ethics Quarterly* 13, no. 4, p. 512.

The Future of Corporate Reporting—Creating the Dynamics for Change. October 2015. Brussels: Federation of European Accountants.

The Rise of the Social Pillar: An Introduction to the "S" in ESG. n.d. CPA Canada, p. 4.

Wall Street. 1987. 20th Century Fox.

Wickert and Risi. 2019. *Corporate Social Responsibility.* University press, Cambridge University, p. 6.

Wickert and Risi. July 2019. "Corporate Social Responsibility, Cambridge Elements." Cambridge University Press.

Wickert and Risi. n.d. p. 8.

Wickert and Risi. n.d. p. 86.

Wickert, C. and D. Risi. July 2019. *Corporate Social Responsibility,* 16. Cambridge University Press.

About the Author

Gerald Trites is a Chartered Professional Accountant and Economics major. He is also a retired partner of KPMG, where he worked extensively on corporate disclosure and strategic planning. In this book, he applies these skills to show how a company can use the experience it gains in providing sustainability disclosures to the development of corporate strategies that extend beyond sustainability to a broader corporate social responsibiity, all without sacrificing profitability.

Index

Note: Letter '*f*' and 'a' after locators indicate figure and appendix, respectively.

www.ingramcontent.com/pod-product-compliance
Lightning Source LLC
Jackson TN
JSHW011351060225
78554JS00007B/268